Norihiro Yagi won the 32nd Akatsuka Award for his debut work, *UNDEADMAN*, which appeared in *Monthly Shonen Jump* magazine and produced two sequels. His first serialized manga was his comedy *Angel Densetsu* (Angel Legend), which appeared in *Monthly Shonen Jump* from 1992 to 2000. His epic saga, *Claymore*, has been running in the magazine since 2001.

In his spare time, Yagi enjoys things like the Japanese comedic duo Downtown, martial arts, games, driving, and hard rock music, but he doesn't consider these actual hobbies.

CLAYMORE VOL. 8
The SHONEN JUMP ADVANCED Manga Edition

STORY AND ART BY
NORIHIRO YAGI

English Adaptation & Translation/Arashi Productions
Touch-up Art & Lettering/Sabrina Heep
Design/Izumi Evers
Editor/Jonathan Tarbox

Editor in Chief, Books/Alvin Lu
Editor in Chief, Magazines/Marc Weidenbaum
VP, Publishing Licensing/Rika Inouye
VP, Sales & Product Marketing/Gonzalo Ferreyra
VP, Creative/Linda Espinosa
Publisher/Hyoe Narita

CLAYMORE © 2001 by Norihiro Yagi. All rights reserved. First published in Japan in 2001 by SHUEISHA Inc., Tokyo. English translation rights arranged by SHUEISHA Inc. The stories, characters and incidents mentioned in this publication are entirely fictional.

No portion of this book may be reproduced or transmitted in any form or by any means without written permission from the copyright holders.

The rights of the author(s) of the work(s) in this publication to be so identified have been asserted in accordance with the Copyright, Designs and Patents Act 1988. A CIP catalogue record for this book is available from the British Library.

Printed in the U.S.A.

Published by VIZ Media, LLC
P.O. Box 77010
San Francisco, CA 94107

SHONEN JUMP ADVANCED Manga Edition
10 9 8 7 6 5 4 3 2
First printing, June 2007
Second printing, September 2008

www.viz.com

RATED T+ FOR OLDER TEEN

PARENTAL ADVISORY
CLAYMORE is rated T+ for Older Teen and is recommended for ages 16 and up. This volume contains realistic violence.
ratings.viz.com

THE WORLD'S MOST CUTTING-EDGE MANGA
SHONEN JUMP ADVANCED
www.shonenjump.com

SHONEN JUMP ADVANCED Manga Edition

クレイモア

Claymore

Vol. 8
The Witch's Maw

Story and Art by Norihiro Yagi

came to be called Claymores after the immense broadswords that they carried.

After losing her right arm to Ophelia, Clare is rescued by the former number 2, Ilena. Can Clare defeat Ophelia using the Quick-Sword technique?

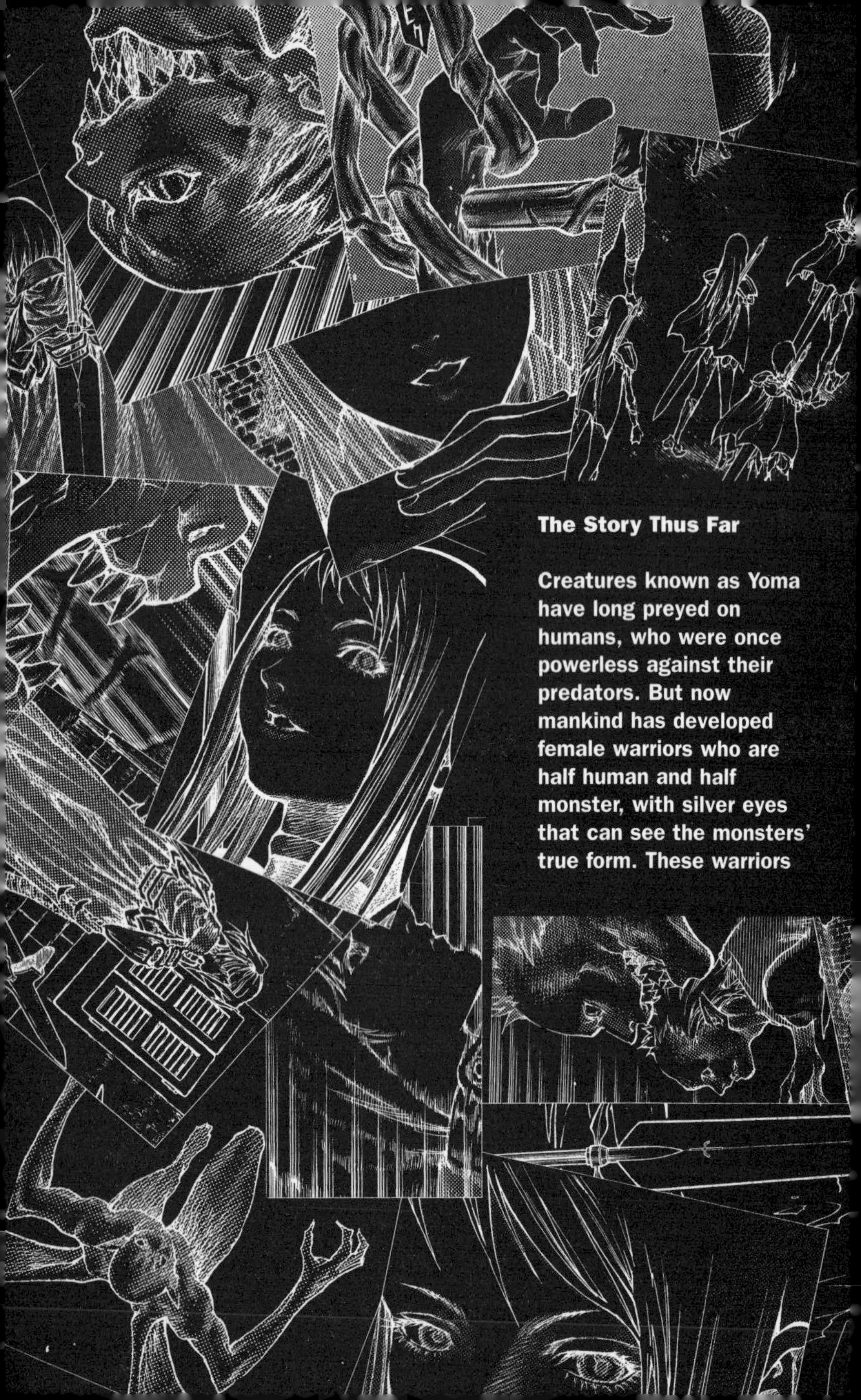

The Story Thus Far

Creatures known as Yoma have long preyed on humans, who were once powerless against their predators. But now mankind has developed female warriors who are half human and half monster, with silver eyes that can see the monsters' true form. These warriors

クレイモア

Claymore™

Vol. 8

CONTENTS

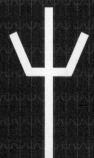

Scene 40: Fit for Battle, Part 4

DAM

BA
Scene 40: Fit for Battle, Part 4

GAAAA
TCH!
DOBAAAT
AGH ...
GAK

DOBABA BA
BABA BA
CHING
CHA CHA CHACHA
HYAAH!
VOOM
FWOOSH

DOGAAAAA
TMP
!

GRAH!
DADA
YOU BITCH!
GASHA GAGAGAGA
!!!

GA
SHUK
GAH ...
SPLASH
NO ...
YOU ...
FWOSH

SPLASH
BIKI
BIKI
BIKI
BIKI
WHA ...
!

UGH ...
BAS HAA
DID I MISTAKE MY LIMITS?
NO... I'M STILL NOT USED TO USING ILENA'S ARM.
BIKI
BIKI
BIKI
BIKI
DOBAAAAA
AH, THAT'S IT...
YOU BOR-ROWED THAT.
I THOUGHT I'D SEEN IT SOMEWHERE BEFORE.

READ THIS WAY

IT'S THE RIGHT ARM ...
...OF THAT NASTY LITTLE WOMAN.
SO THAT'S HOW YOU GOT SO STRONG IN SUCH A SHORT TIME.
GRR ...
BKI
BKI
GRIP
HUFF
HUFF
HUFF
ZAAA
HUFF
YOU'RE RE-LEASING YOUR POWER INTO JUST ONE ARM.
THAT MEANS YOU HAVE TO CONTROL THAT ARM WITHOUT LETTING THE SWORD SLIP FROM YOUR GRASP, RIGHT?
IT'S TOO MUCH FOR YOU.
THAT FOREIGN ARM IS THROWING YOUR WHOLE BODY OFF.

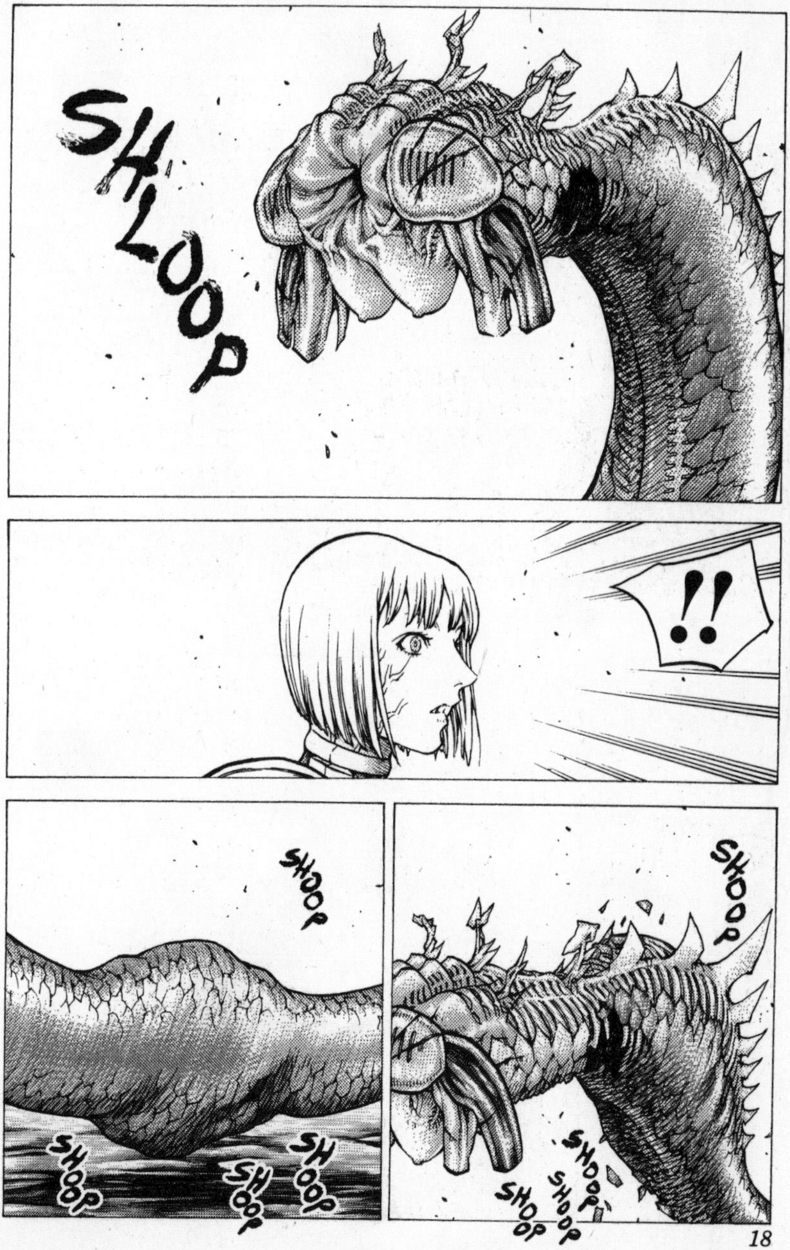

18

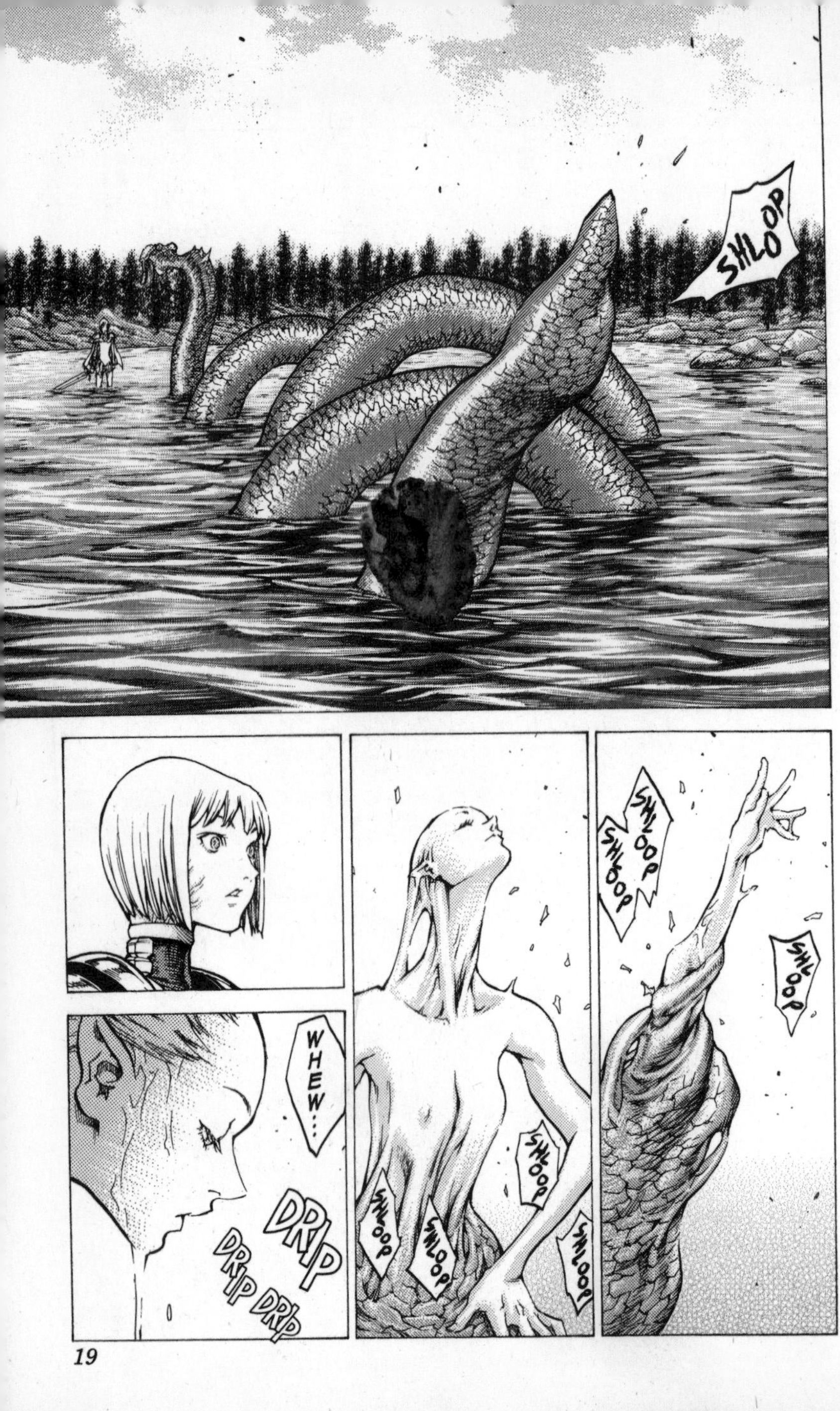
SHLOP
SHLOOP
SHLOOP
SHLOOP
SHLOOP
SHLOOP
SHLOOP
SHLOOP
WHEW...
DRIP
DRIP DRIP DRIP

I'VE CONCENTRATED THE PART OF ME THAT'S STILL HUMAN IN MY TAIL.
IN OTHER WORDS, THIS IS MY WEAK POINT.
DRIP
DRIP
NOW LET'S PLAY A LITTLE GAME.
IF YOU CAN CUT PAST ALL THE REST OF ME AND GET HERE, YOU WIN.

INTER-ESTING GAME, DON'T YOU THINK?

IT MEANS YOU'RE NOT FIT TO BATTLE THAT ONE-HORNED MONSTER.

BUT IF HALFWAY THROUGH YOU GO PAST YOUR LIMITS AND AWAKEN, THEN *I WIN.*

IF I LOSE ...

I'LL SUBMIT OBEDI-ENTLY TO YOUR WILL.

HUFF

BIKI BIKI BIKI

HUFF

HUFF

BIKI

BIKI

BIKI

BA
DA
DOGA
AAA

AND YOU HAVEN'T THOUGHT ABOUT THE FEELINGS OF THOSE WHO WERE LEFT BEHIND.

THAT PRIDE WILL GET YOU KILLED.

I WONDER WHY YOU'RE SO DESPERATE...

YOU SHOULD IGNORE WHAT I SAY AND TRY TO STRIKE RIGHT HERE.

YOU'RE SO FOOLISH.

I WONDER WHY I SAID THAT?

HM?

GET AWAY! HURRY!

GO NOW!

THERE'S NO WAY HE COULD WIN. WHY DID HE TRY SUCH HEROICS?

A FOOLISH GESTURE, REALLY.

MY BROTHER TRIED TO SAVE ME BY FIGHTING THAT THING.

AH... THAT'S RIGHT...

GET OUT OF HERE WHILE YOU STILL CAN!

I'LL HOLD THIS THING OFF!

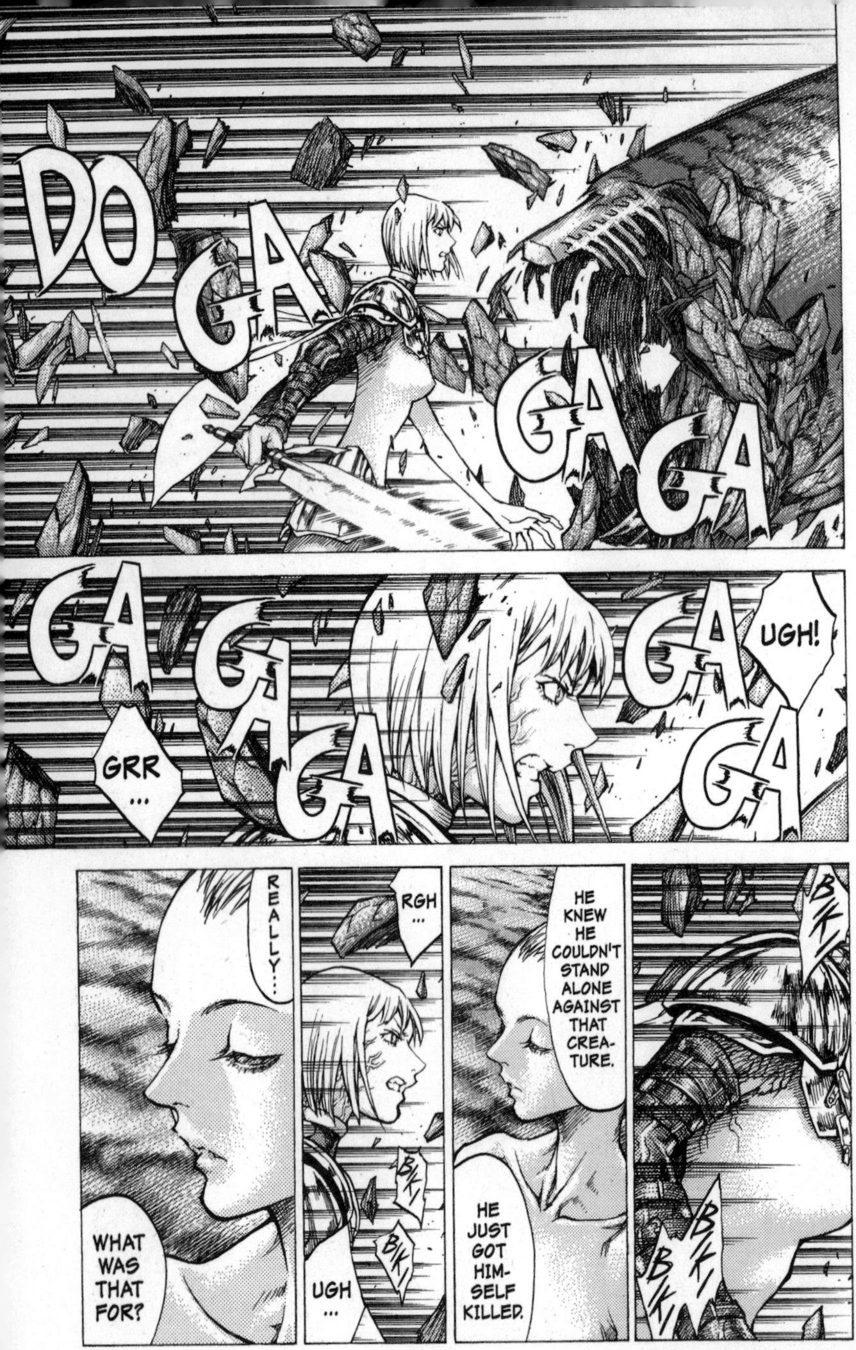

25

KA
THUK
AH ...
AAAGH!

READ THIS WAY

AGH ...
GAH!
FINISHED ALREADY, ARE WE?
JUST AS I EX-PECTED.
GUAA
DAMN!
MOVE...
MOVE...
MOVE...
MOVE...
DAMN IT.
BIKI
BIKI
DAMN IT.
DAMN IT.
MOVE ... YOUR ARM ...
BIKI
BIKI

WHAT THE HELL ARE YOU DO-ING!?
IF YOU GO GET YOUR-SELF KILLED, WHAT ABOUT THE ONES YOU LEAVE BEHIND!?
BIKI
BIKI
BIKI
BIKI
BIKI
WHAM

DO GAGAGA
GA
GA GA GA GA
WHAT'S THIS?
YOU CAN DO IT IF YOU TRY.
!
GAGAGA
GA
HM?
WHY AM I TRYING TO HELP THIS GIRL?
GA GA GA GA

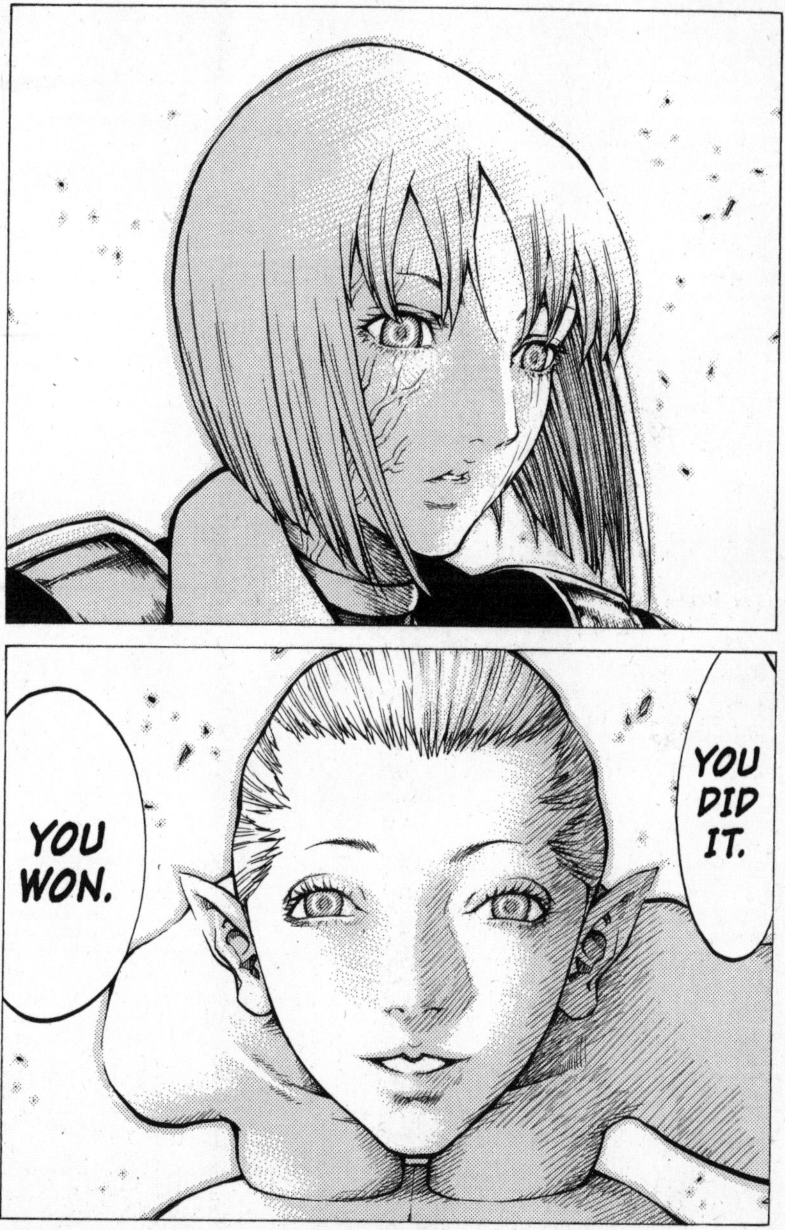
YOU DID IT.
YOU WON.

READ THIS WAY

AND AS I PROMISED, I YIELD EVERY-THING TO YOU.
THERE WAS NOTHING I COULD HAVE DONE, ANYWAY.
I REALLY HATE THEM.
PEOPLE LIKE YOU WHO RISK THEIR LIVES SO SELF-ISHLY— I HATE THEM.
HURRY UP AND FINISH ME OFF.
IF YOU DON'T HURRY, I'LL REGEN-ERATE.

THUK
IF YOU'RE GOING TO FIGHT IN MY PLACE ...
I WON'T FORGIVE YOU IF YOU LOSE.

READ THIS WAY

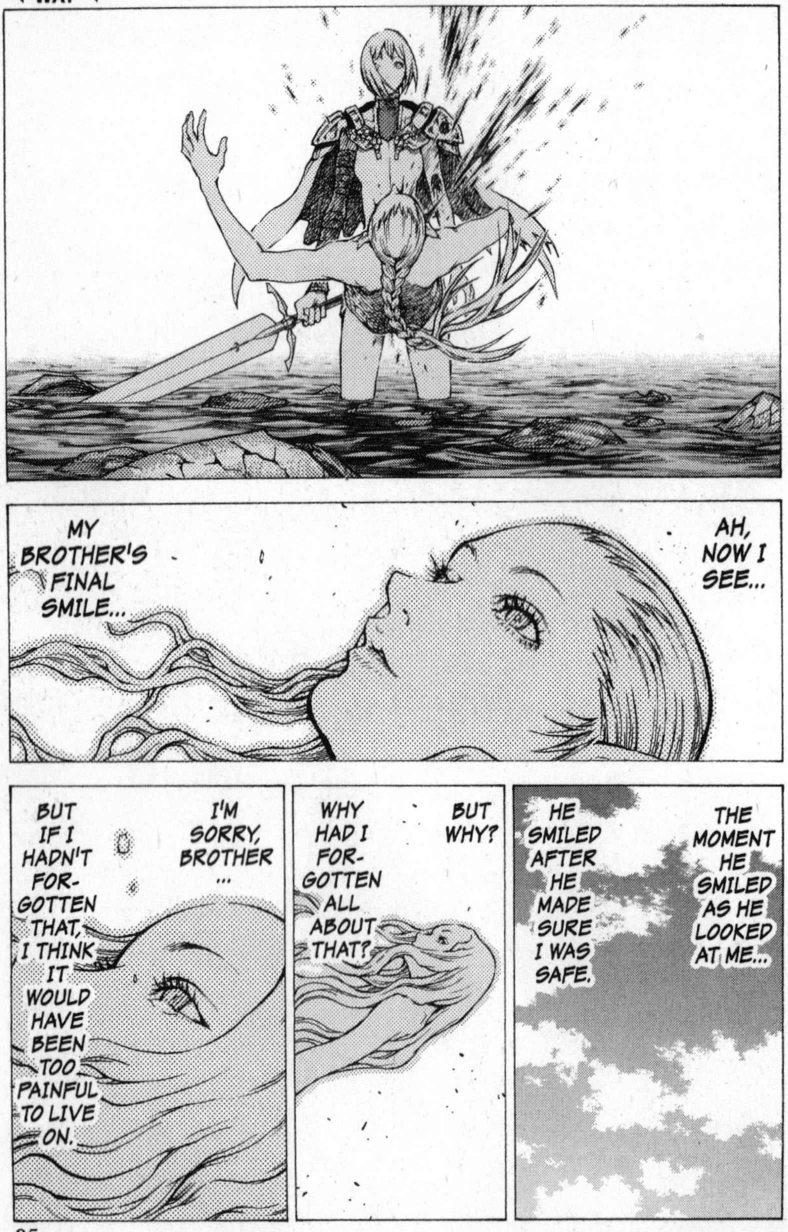

AH, NOW I SEE...
MY BROTHER'S FINAL SMILE...
THE MOMENT HE SMILED AS HE LOOKED AT ME...
HE SMILED AFTER HE MADE SURE I WAS SAFE.
BUT WHY?
WHY HAD I FOR-GOTTEN ALL ABOUT THAT?
I'M SORRY, BROTHER...
BUT IF I HADN'T FOR-GOTTEN THAT, I THINK IT WOULD HAVE BEEN TOO PAINFUL TO LIVE ON.

I'LL SEE YOU IN THE NEXT WORLD...
WE'LL BE TOGETHER AGAIN...

Scene 41: The Witch's
Maw, Part 1

READ THIS WAY
WSSH...
THE FAR EAST LAND OF SUTAFU
YOU'VE LOST CONTACT WITH NUMBER 47?

HOW LONG HAS IT BEEN?
THREE MONTHS SINCE MY LAST CON-TACT.
HER LAST MIS-SION?
HUNT-ING AN AWAKENED ONE IN THE VILLAGE OF GONAHL.
A JOB WITH NUM-BER 4.
IS THERE ANY CHANCE SHE WAS KILLED IN ACTION?
I CAN'T SAY FOR SURE.
BUT HER BODY WASN'T FOUND.

READ THIS WAY

NUMBER 4... OPHELIA LEFT THE VILLAGE OF GONAHL AND WENT INTO THE MOUNTAINS. HER CORPSE AS AN AWAKENED ONE WAS DISCOVERED.
IS THERE A CHANCE THAT NUMBER 47 WAS THE ONE WHO TOOK OPHELIA'S LIFE?
IF YOU'RE ASKING WHETHER NUMBER 47 COULD TAKE ON NUMBER 4—AND AN AWAKENED 4 AT THAT—BY HERSELF AND WIN...
WE'D HAVE TO SAY THE POSSI-BILITY IS PRAC-TICALLY ZERO.
ORDI-NARILY IT WOULD BE IMPOS-SIBLE ...
BUT THE RANK NUMBER ALONE IS NOT NECES-SARILY A PERFECT MEASURE OF STRENGTH.
AFTER ALL, THE FLESH OF TERE-SA...
...MAY WELL HAVE MADE NUMBER 47 SOME-THING QUITE SPECIAL.

IT WAS AN ATTEMPT TO CONTINUE THE STRENGTH OF A SUPERBLY GIFTED WARRIOR BY TRANS-PLANTING ITS FLESH INTO A NEW RECRUIT.
HOWEVER, WASN'T IT DETERMINED TO BE UNSUCCESS-FUL?
LOOKING ONLY AT THE NUMBERS, THAT CON-CLUSION WAS REACHED.
AT PRESENT, THERE'S NO DOUBT THAT NUMBER 47 HAS SOME UNDETERMINED FACTORS.
EITHER WAY, WE CAN'T JUST LEAVE IT THAT WE DON'T KNOW WHETHER SHE'S ALIVE OR DEAD.
IF SHE'S STILL ALIVE, WE HAVE TO SEARCH HER OUT.
ERMITA.
SIR?
GIVE THIS JOB TO HER.
IT'S A TOP PRIORITY. GIVE IT PRECE-DENCE OVER ALL HER OTHERS.

READ THIS WAY

UNDER-STOOD.
IF THEY CALLED ERMITA, THAT MEANS IT'S HER TIME.
I SEE. SHE'S PERFECT FOR IT.
HEH HEH HEH.
THE SITUATION MUST BE DESPERATE...
I WONDER WHAT SHE'S UP TO?

EXCUSE ME. I'M LOOKING FOR MY BROTHER.
HAVE YOU SEEN A YOUNG LAD WANDERING ALONE IN THIS VILLAGE RECENTLY?
!
I DON'T RECALL SUCH. BUT LOTS OF FOLKS HAVE BEEN PASSING THROUGH RECENTLY.
A YOUNG FELLAH LIKE THAT WOULDN'T DRAW MUCH NOTICE.
IT'S A LARGE VILLAGE. IF YOU LOOK AROUND, YOU MIGHT FIND HIM.
HOPE YOU FIND HIM, BUDDY.
THANK YOU.

READ THIS WAY
YOU CLOD! THAT WAS A GIRL, NOT A BOY.
WHAT ARE YOU TALKING ABOUT? HE WAS CARRY-ING A HUGE SWORD, WASN'T HE?
AND HE HAD A MAN'S VOICE.
TMP
TMP
IF I STRETCH MY VOCAL CHORDS...
MAYBE I CAN MAKE IT GO DEEPER.
GU GU

RAKI!...

WHERE THE DEVIL ARE YOU?

I'LL BE STAYING A WHILE.

YES, A ROOM, PLEASE.

A ROOM FOR ONE?

WEL-COME, FRIEND!

GACHAK

IF YAH WAS TO SEARCH EVERY CORNER OF THE TOWN...

RATTLE

CAN'T SAY FOR SURE. IT'S A MIGHTY BIG TOWN.

PERHAPS YOU'VE SEEN HIM?

I'M LOOKING FOR MY BROTHER WHO GOT LOST DURING OUR TRAVELS.

BETTER LET YAH KNOW...

OH, AND ONE THING...

...THERE'S A GROUP O' THEM CLAYMORES STAYING.

HERE IN THIS TOWN...

AN AWAKENED ONE...

WORD IS HE'S PRETTY TOUGH, SO THERE'S FOUR OF 'EM COME TO GET 'EM.

THEY SAY THERE'S A YOMA IN THE MOUNTAINS NEARBY.

THANKS FOR THE WARNING.

DON'T BE SURPRISED IF YAH BUMP INTO THEM IN THE STREET.

THEY SAY THEM CLAYMORES NEVER LAY A HAND ON REGULAR FOLK, BUT I THOUGHT I OUGHTA TELL YA.

WHEW.

CLUNK

BATAN

CREAK

READ THIS WAY

PLINK
I DON'T HAVE MANY LEFT OF THE PILLS I RECEIVED TO SUPPRESS MY YOMA AURA.
THANKS TO THEM, I CAN PASS WITHOUT PEOPLE OR WARRIORS TELLING WHAT I AM.
BUT WITH THESE PILLS, WHILE I DON'T PROJECT A YOMA AURA, I ALSO CAN'T SENSE ANY YOMA AURAS NEARBY.
AS I AM NOW, I COULDN'T SPOT A YOMA IF IT WAS STANDING RIGHT NEXT TO ME.
SO WHILE TRYING TO AVOID MY COMRADES, I WALKED RIGHT INTO A VILLAGE FULL OF THEM.
DAMN...
KLAK
MR MR
MR MR
SHAK
MRMR
MRMR
MRMR
!

CLANK CLANK
CLANK
IF THEY'RE HUNTING AN AWAKENED ONE, AT LEAST ONE OF THEM HAS TO BE A SINGLE DIGIT.
BUT WHICH ONE?
AND SPEAK OF THE DEVIL...
CLANK
CLANK
CLANK

READ THIS WAY

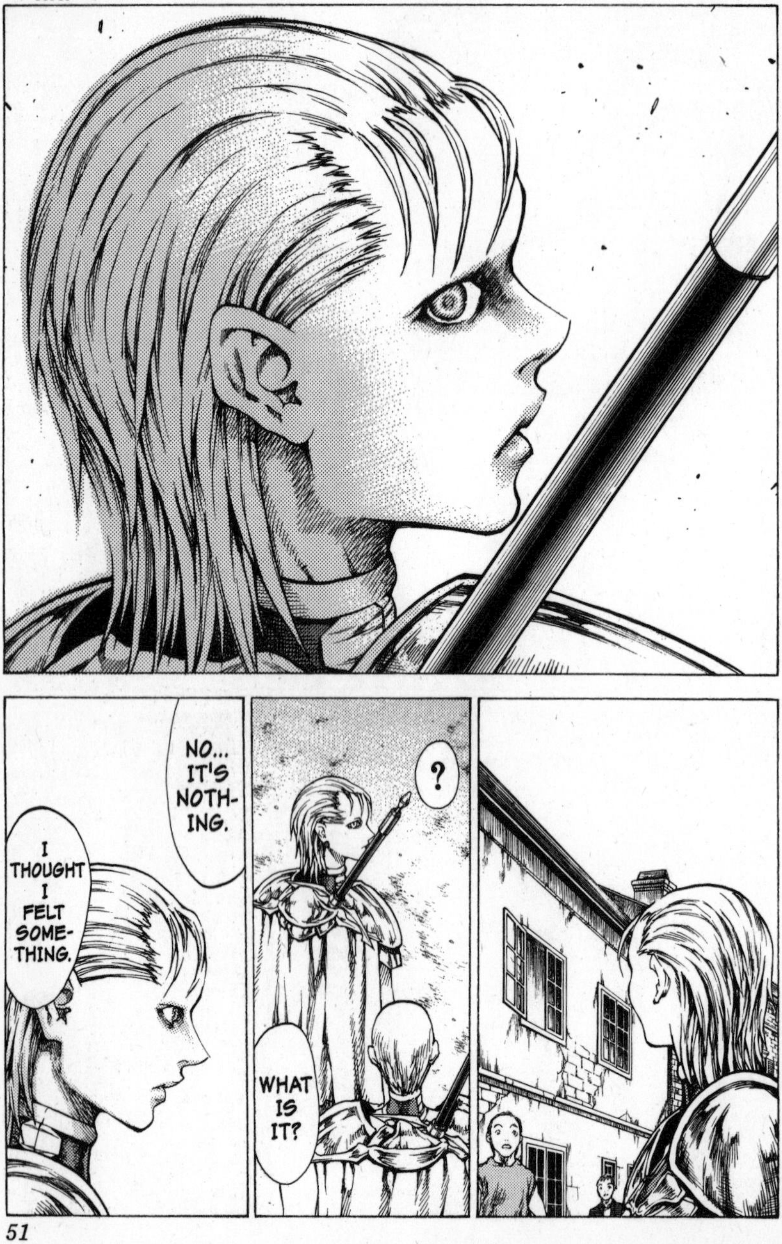
?
WHAT IS IT?
NO... IT'S NOTHING.
I THOUGHT I FELT SOMETHING.

SHE MUST BE THE SINGLE DIGIT.

THAT ONE.

...AND NONE OF THEM KNOW MY FACE, SO I SHOULD BE SAFE.

EITHER WAY, I'M DISGUISED LIKE THIS...

IS SHE ONE OF THE TOP FIVE?

OR A LOWER NUMBER?

IN MY CURRENT STATE, THERE'S NO WAY I CAN ASSESS THEIR STRENGTH.

READ THIS WAY

SHHP
NOW THEN ...
I DON'T WANT TO RUN INTO THEM IF I CAN AVOID IT.
BUT I DON'T HAVE MUCH TIME.
CLANK

GATATAT
OH... MORNIN'.
YER UP MIGHT EARLY.
YES.
I WANTED TO GET STARTED SEARCHING FOR MY BROTHER.
OH, I SEE.
BY THE WAY... THE CLAYMORE BUNCH I TOLD YAH ABOUT TOOK OFF EARLY THIS MORNIN'.
HUNTING AFTER THAT YOMA.
!
ALL FOUR OF 'EM LEFT BEFORE SUN-UP.
KINDA GLAD THEY'RE GONE, TOO.
EVEN IF THEY ARE HALF HUMAN, THEY'RE STILL PART YOMA, TOO.
THE ONLY MOUNTAINS NEAR HERE ARE THE ZAKOL.
THAT'S NOT TOO FAR.
BUT EVEN WITH AN EASY VICTORY, IT'LL TAKE AT LEAST A DAY.
I'M OFF. I MIGHT NOT BE BACK UNTIL NIGHTFALL.
CREAK
ALL RIGHTY. HOPE YAH FIND YER BROTHER.

« READ THIS WAY «

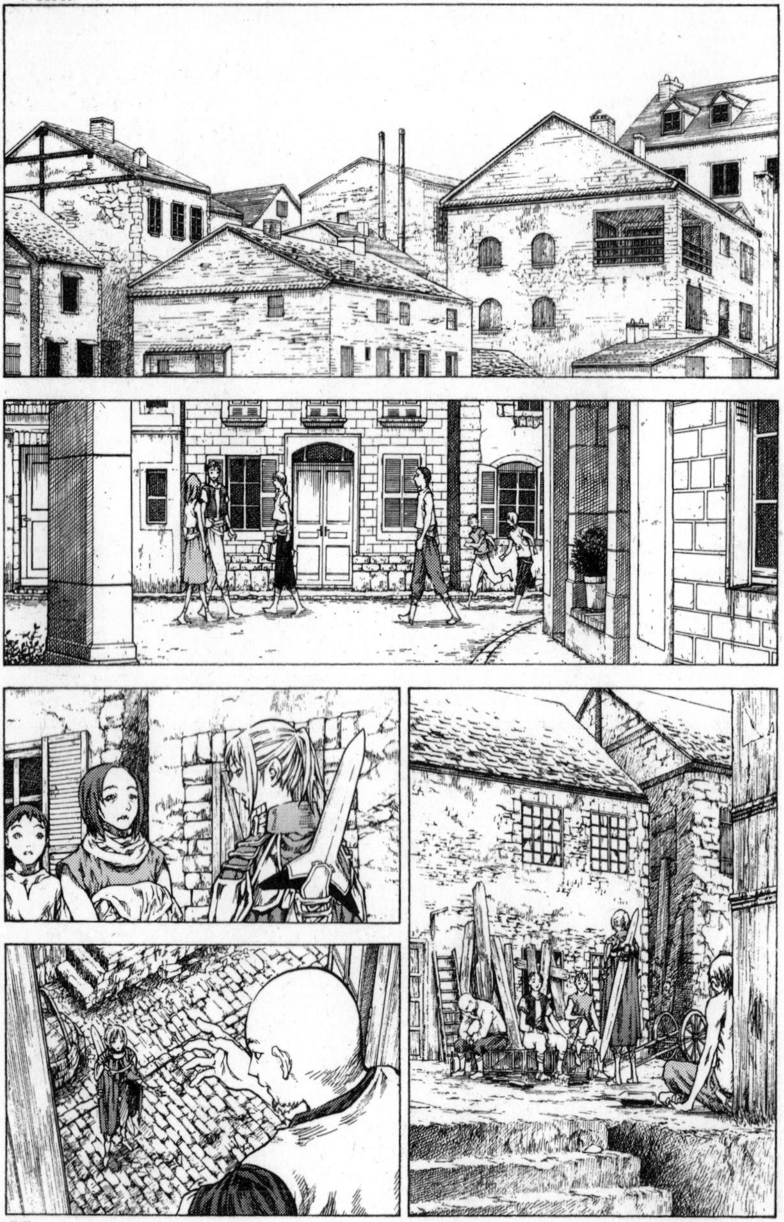

NO SIGN OF HIM AT ALL.
SINCE WE SPLIT UP, I'VE SEARCHED EVERY VILLAGE NEAR THAT MOUNTAIN, BUT HAVEN'T FOUND A TRACE.
RAKI...
WHERE DID YOU...
!
WOW! IT'S TERESA AND CLARE!
THEY CALL THESE TWO TERESA AND CLARE!
WHAT!?

"MAYBE YOU WERE NAMED THAT IN HOPES THAT YOU WOULD BE RAISED TO BECOME LIKE THAT."

"THE NAMES OF TWIN GODDESSES... BEAUTIFUL AND PURE, OVER-FLOWING WITH ABUNDANT LOVE.

I KNEW ALL THAT BEFORE YOU TOLD ME!

AH, YOU HEARD THAT FROM ME JUST A LITTLE WHILE AGO.

NO! THAT GUY WAS JUST BEGGIN' ME TO TELL HIM WHICH ONE WAS CLARE'S STATUE.

THAT'S 'CAUSE THAT STRANGER TOLD YOU ABOUT IT.

WHAT KIND OF BOY WAS HE?

THAT'S ALL RIGHT.

YEAH, BUT I DIDN'T KNOW THE GUY.

COULD YOU TELL ME WHO YOU WERE JUST TALKING ABOUT?

EX- CUSE ME, CHILD.

ALL BEAT UP WITH WOUNDS... HE SORTA SCARED ME AT FIRST.

HE WAS ALL RAG- GEDY.

READ THIS WAY

BUT WHEN HE HEARD ABOUT THE IMAGE OF CLARE, HIS EYES GOT ALL SOFT AND GENTLE.
THEN I WASN'T SCARED, SO I KEPT TALKING TO HIM.
DO YOU KNOW WHERE HE WENT?
UH... NO, I DON'T.
I HAVEN'T SEEN HIM IN THIS VILLAGE SINCE THEN.
ALL RIGHT. THANK YOU.
HEY.
DO YOU KNOW THAT GUY, MISTER?
UH... HE'S MY BRO...
!
...

NO ... HE'S VERY IMPOR- TANT TO ME.
I CARE ABOUT HIM SO MUCH THAT I PROMISED I'D FIND HIM EVEN IF I HAD TO RISK MY LIFE.
THAT'S GREAT. I HOPE YOU FIND HIM SOON.
THANKS.

READ
THIS
WAY

GACH
AK

GACHAK
GACHAK
!

GYAH!!
CHAK
CHAK
WH ...
WHAT THE ...?
MRMR
MR MR

READ THIS WAY

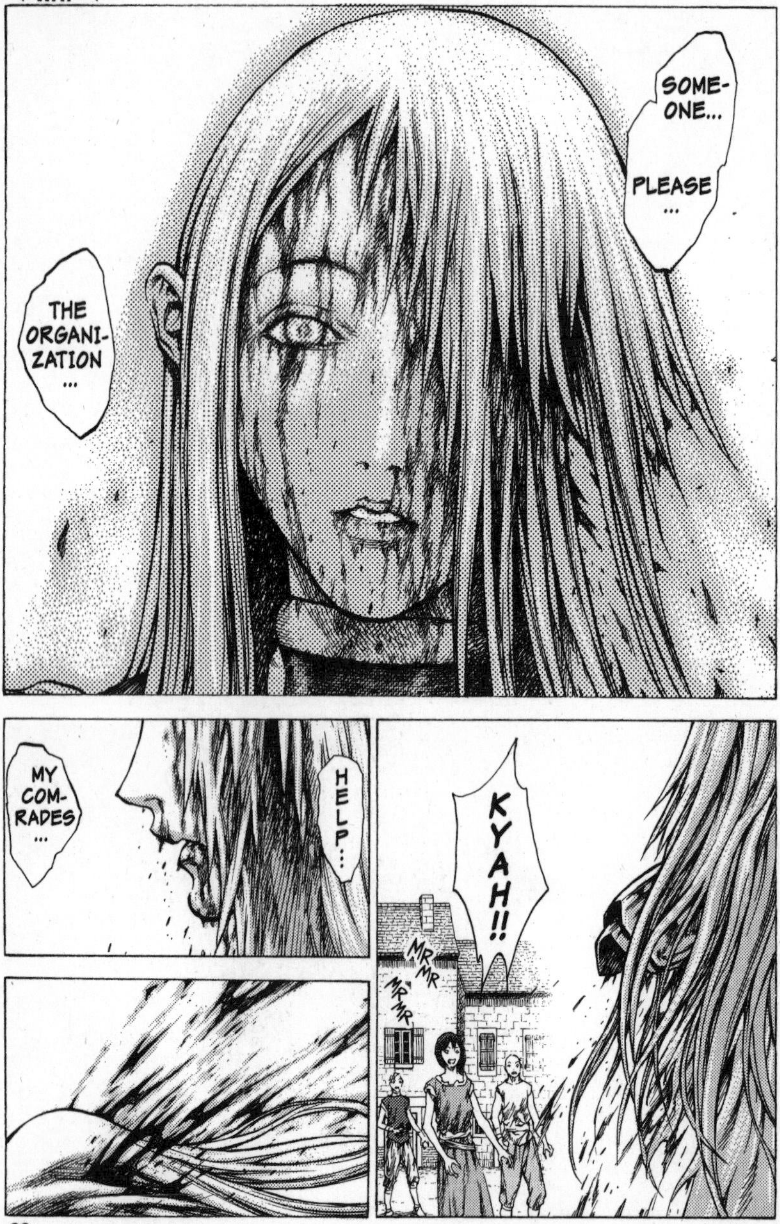

KA
THUD
SPLAT
SPLAT
SPLAT
AH!
UGK...
GUH...
HEY!
SPEAK TO ME!
HEY!

READ THIS WAY

PLEASE...
CON... CONTACT THE ORGANIZATION...
SO STRONG...
SO...
WAS IT AN AWAKENED ONE!?
!
DID AN AWAKENED ONE DO THIS!?
!!
ARE YOU...
...A COMRADE?
GRIP

PLEASE...
SAVE THE OTHERS ...
THEY'RE STILL ... ALIVE ...
SOME-THING'S STRANGE... THEY WANT TO TAKE US ALIVE... THEY'RE PLOTTING SOME-THING...
PLEASE...
THE OTHERS ...
HELP THEM ...
HEL ...

READ THIS WAY
SLUMP
URGH ...

KASH

KAK

IF POSSIBLE, I'D LIKE YOU TO GIVE IT A DECENT HUMAN FUNERAL.

PLEASE TAKE CARE OF THE BODY.

... COMRADES?

YOUR...

THAT WOULDN'T BE RIGHT.

BUSHA

EVEN IF I HAVE GONE INTO HIDING, I CAN'T JUST SIT BACK AND WATCH MY COMRADES BE MURDERED.

WHAT DO YOU THINK YOU'RE DOING WITH THAT SWORD, YOUNG FELLAH?

YOU'RE NOT GOING INTO THE MOUNTAINS, ARE YOU? YOU'RE JUST GONNA GET YOURSELF KILLED!

GA SHAK
I'M CLARE, NUMBER 47.
I'M GOING TO SUPPORT THE HUNT FOR THE AWAKENED ONE IN ZAKOL.

クレイモア
Claymore™

SCENE 42: THE WITCH'S MAW, PART 2

Scene 42: The Witch's Maw, Part 2
WHOOK

KA

THUD
THUD
THUD
YOU ...
YOU'RE...
...A CLAY-MORE, EH?
BIKI
BIKI
BIKI
BIKI
BIKI
BA
BASH

READ THIS WAY

GRAAH!!

!!

YOU'RE DEAD!

BUT EVEN YOU GUYS CAN'T FACE A MULTIPLE ATTACK IN THE AIR.

MAYBE YOU THOUGHT YOU COULD HUNT US WITHOUT MUCH TROUBLE, I GUESS.

IF ONE OF US GOES AT THE FEET AND ANOTHER AT THE TRUNK, YOUR KIND ALWAYS LEAPS IN THE AIR.

BIKI

GRAAH!!

GASHAK
HUH!?
AGH.
GAH ...

THUMP
SPLAT
SPLAT
SPLAT
YOU...
...BITCH!
SHWAK

READ THIS WAY

EH?
YOU'VE GOT TOO MUCH LEADER-SHIP.
IT ISN'T LIKE YOU.
WHAT ARE YOU UP TO?
HEH HEH HEH.
LAUGH WHILE YOU CAN.
YOU'RE JUST LIKE THE OTHERS.
GO THERE AND FIND OUT FOR YOUR-SELF.
YOU'RE A FOOL SEEK-ING YOUR OWN DEATH.
DOBAT

FWSH
GASHAKN
YOMA IN GROUPS FOLLOWING ORDERS, COORDINATING WITH TWO FLIERS ...
...USING STRATEGY BASED ON OUR REACTIONS...
WHY?
WHAT THE HELL IS GOING ON?

READ THIS WAY

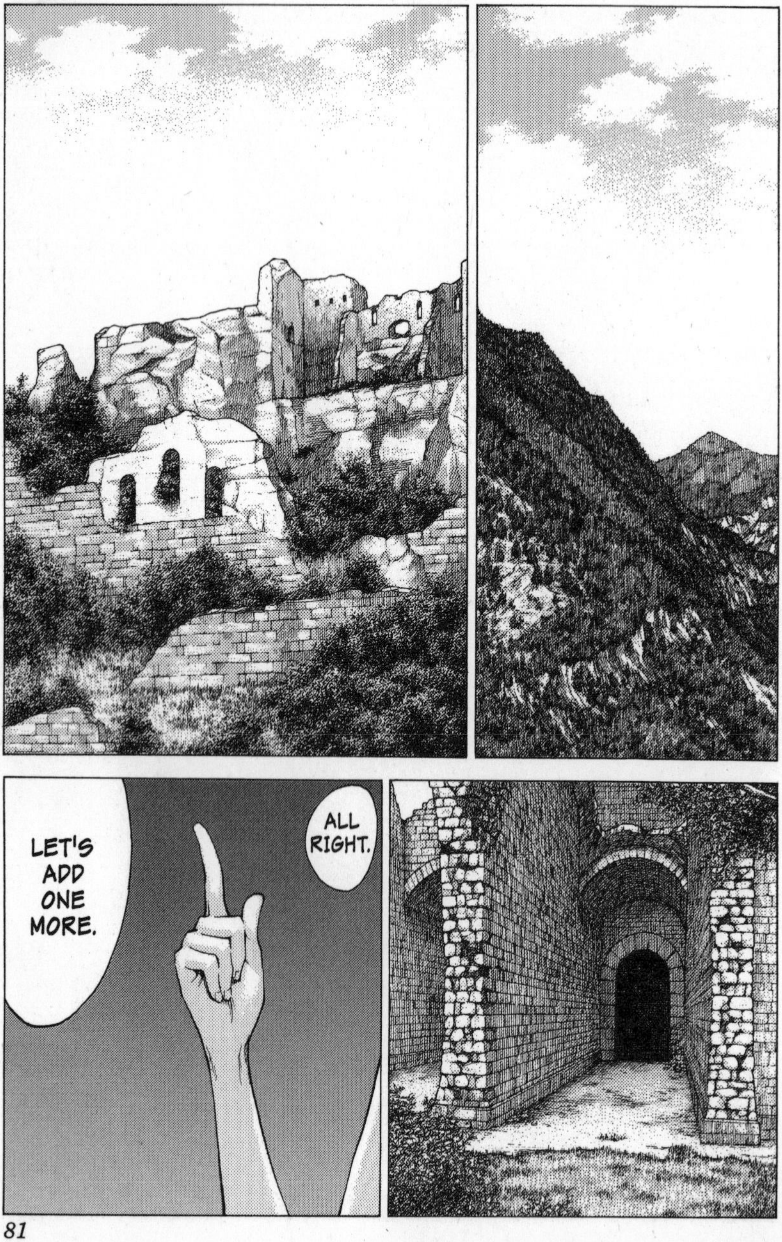
ALL RIGHT.
LET'S ADD ONE MORE.

GYEH!
POK
GRIP
POK
POK
POK
POK
POK
SHLOK

READ THIS WAY

I EXPECTED YOU'D WANT TO AWAKEN BY NOW.

UGH ...
UG ...
UG ...
GYEH HEH.
SLURP
!!
TWIST
TWIST
TWIST
GAH!
GAHA!
UGH GA HA!
TOUGH, AREN'T YOU?
IF YOU DON'T HURRY UP AND AWAKEN, YOU END UP FULL OF HOLES AND DEAD, LIKE THAT ONE OVER THERE.
DON'T YOU CARE?

READ THIS WAY

YOU ...
YOU ...
AH!
AH!
AH!
!
GAH...
BIKI
GAH ...
GAH ...
GAH ...
GAH ...
BIKI
BIKI
BIKI
STOP IT!
DON'T DO IT, KATEA!
WELL, NOW!
THAT'S THE WAY.
ONCE YOU AWAKEN, ALL YOUR WOUNDS WILL HEAL AND YOUR PAIN WILL VANISH.

AGH!

THWOK

DO YOU WANT TO BECOME A MON-STER!?

STOP IT, KATEA!

DON'T INSULT US LIKE THAT.

WHO YOU CALLIN' A MON-STER?

DON'T PUT ANY MORE IN TILL I TELL YOU.

HEY, WHAT ARE YOU DOING?

BUT SHE...

...ARE THE ONES I KILL FIRST!

THE ONES WHO INSULT US...

BIKI

BIKI

BIKI

FWOM
!!!
THAT'S IT!
SHE'S PAST HER LIMITS.
GAH.
GAH.
GAH.
GAH.

BOK
BOK
GRA GA GA GA!
GAH. GAH. GAH.
BOK BOK BOK
KATEA...
NOW... REMOVE THE MANA-CLES.
RIGHT!
GET READY, DAUF!
FWOM
!!!

BOK
BOK BOK BOK BOK
BOK BOK
WH...
WHAT...
WHAT ARE YOU DO-ING?
GAH.
GAH.
GAH.
GRAH.
GAH.
GAH.
GAH.

OOOH
GRAK
GEK
GEK
GEK

GOOO
AH...
GAH.
AH...

WHAK
GWOH
GEH ...
GAH ... AH...
!!!

GAH!
FWOOSH
DOGAAT
HMM.
WELL, DAUF?
HOW IS IT?

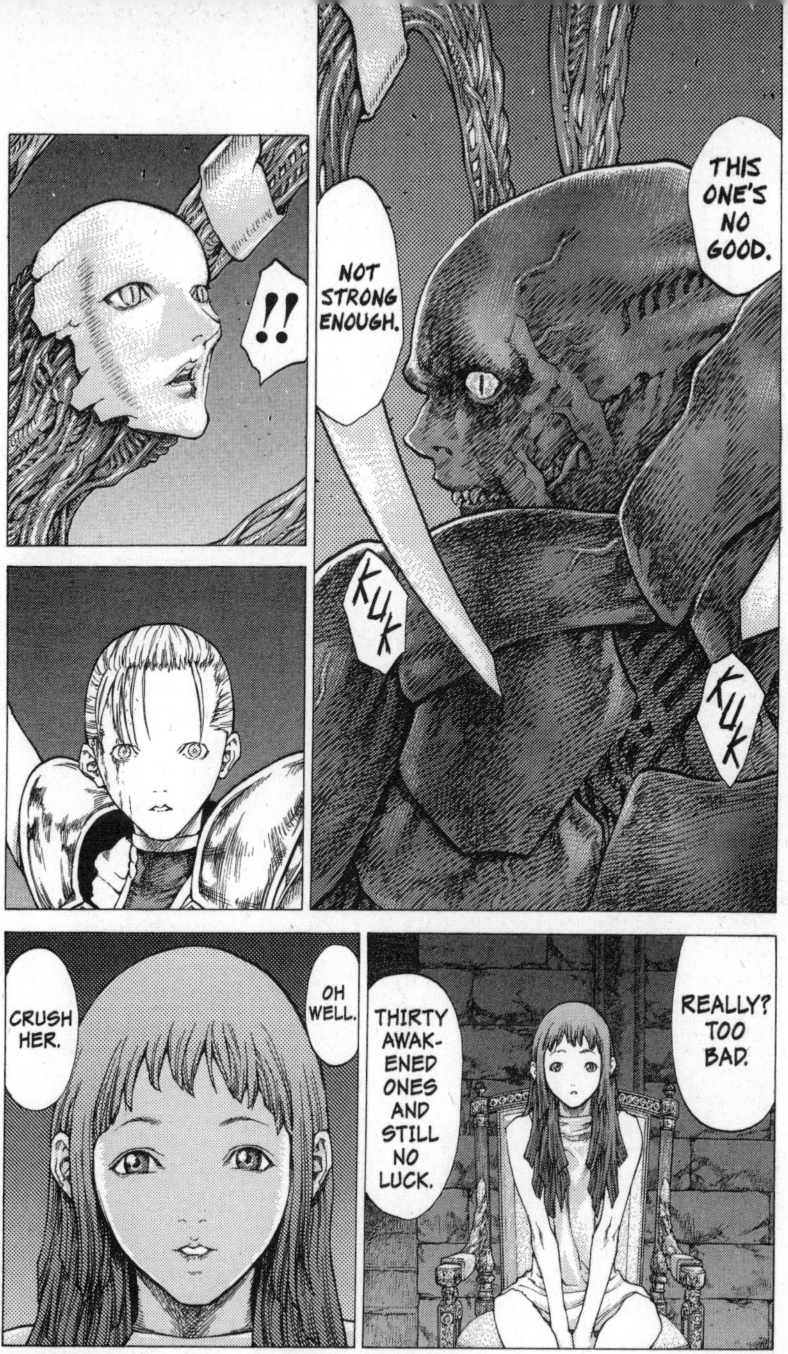
THIS ONE'S NO GOOD.
NOT STRONG ENOUGH.
KUK KUK
!!
REALLY? TOO BAD.
THIRTY AWAK-ENED ONES AND STILL NO LUCK.
OH WELL.
CRUSH HER.

GAH
S...STOP!
KATEA!

DOGAAAT
CRACK
CRACK
CRACK
SO ...
I GUESS I WAS RIGHT. ONLY A ONE-DIGIT LIKE YOURSELF WILL DO.

READ THIS WAY

GLINT
SOME-BODY'S COMIN'.
!
YOU'RE RIGHT.
THAT ONE WHO ESCAPED MANAGED TO CALL HELP PRETTY FAST.
BUT THIS ONE'S GOT AN AWFULLY WEAK AURA.
THAT MUST MEAN SHE'S A LOW-NUMBERED WARRIOR WHO WAS PASSING BY.
WE CAN'T EXPECT HER TO AWAK-EN.
YOU CAN HAVE HER, DAUF.
DO WHAT-EVER YOU WANT.

READ THIS WAY

クレイモア
Claymore™

GASHAK

A BUNCH OF YOMA AURAS ARE COMING FROM ALL OVER THE CASTLE.

BUT WHAT'S THIS STRANGE AURA?

THE RUINS OF A CASTLE.

THIS MUST BE THE DUNGEON.

SCENE 43: THE WITCH'S MAW, PART 3

GASHAK
THESE HAVE A PULSE.
SO THAT'S WHY THERE WERE MULTI-PLE AURAS.
SSH...
THROB
THROB
THROB

READ THIS WAY

IS EACH ONE OF THESE A PIECE OF A YOMA'S BODY?
TO INCREASE THE SIZE OF ITS BODY AND PRODUCE THESE THINGS, THIS ONE MUST HAVE MASSIVE ENERGY.
HOW STRONG CAN THIS THING BE?
HYUUU
GASHA!
TWO AURAS ...
YOMA!
WSSH
!!

CHANG
CHANG
THWOK
THWOK
BA BAT
!!
GRAAH!!

READ THIS WAY

TCH!
WITH ALL THE YOMA AURAS AROUND HERE, I DIDN'T SENSE THEM COMING!
A NASTY LITTLE TRICK!
ZUBAT
GASHUT
GA SHAN
CHING
!!
GRAAH!!
FWSH

DAMN!
THESE RODS ARE STOPPING ME FROM SWING-ING MY LONG SWORD.
GRAAAH!!
THOK
FWSH
ZUBAAT
!
DOGAAAAT

READ THIS WAY

GA!
GE!
GU GA!
BIKI
GA GA!
BIKI BIKI
GA!
YOU RAN ...
CAN'T ALLOW THAT.
GA ...
KUK
GA!
KUK KUK KUK
GA!
GE!
GA!
GWA!
GASHU

!
BLOP
BLOP
BLOP
FOOLS...
KRAK
KRAK
I DO SO MUCH TO SET THINGS UP FOR THESE FOOLS, ALL FOR NOTHING.
TINGLE
TINGLE TINGLE
WORTH-LESS FOOLS ...
SPLAT
THE WHOLE LOT OF THEM.
WH-WHAT THE...
THIS AURA IS GIGAN-TIC...

GA GAGA

GA
TINGLE
TINGLE
TINGLE
...
HM?
WHAT'S THIS?
THAT'S A STRANGE OUTFIT ...

SAY... YOU'RE A MAN, ARE YA?
IF YOU'RE A MAN, THERE'S NO USE PLAYING WITH YOU... HOW BORING.
GOGOGO
WELL THEN, I'LL JUST PEEL OFF YOUR CLOTHES AND FIND OUT.
SSH
!
HUH?
!
HUH?
GESH
GESH
HUH?
IT'S SO NAR-ROW HERE.
GESH
GESH
GESH
I CAN'T MOVE.
WSSH

GA
CHAAAN
!!!
OW ...
OW OW OW.

WHAT D'YA DO THAT FOR?
THAT HURT!
GA CHAAN
FSSH
!!

READ THIS WAY

WHAM

KA
ZA
ZAT
GRH!
BWE HE HE HE!
WHAT'S A WAR-RIOR DO WHEN THEY DROP THEIR SWORD?
ACK!
POK

FWISH
GRIP
IT'S A TRAP.
YOU FOOL.
BIKI
SO WAS THIS.
BIKI
HM?
BIKI
BIKI
BIKI
BIKI
BIKI

QUICK-SWORD!

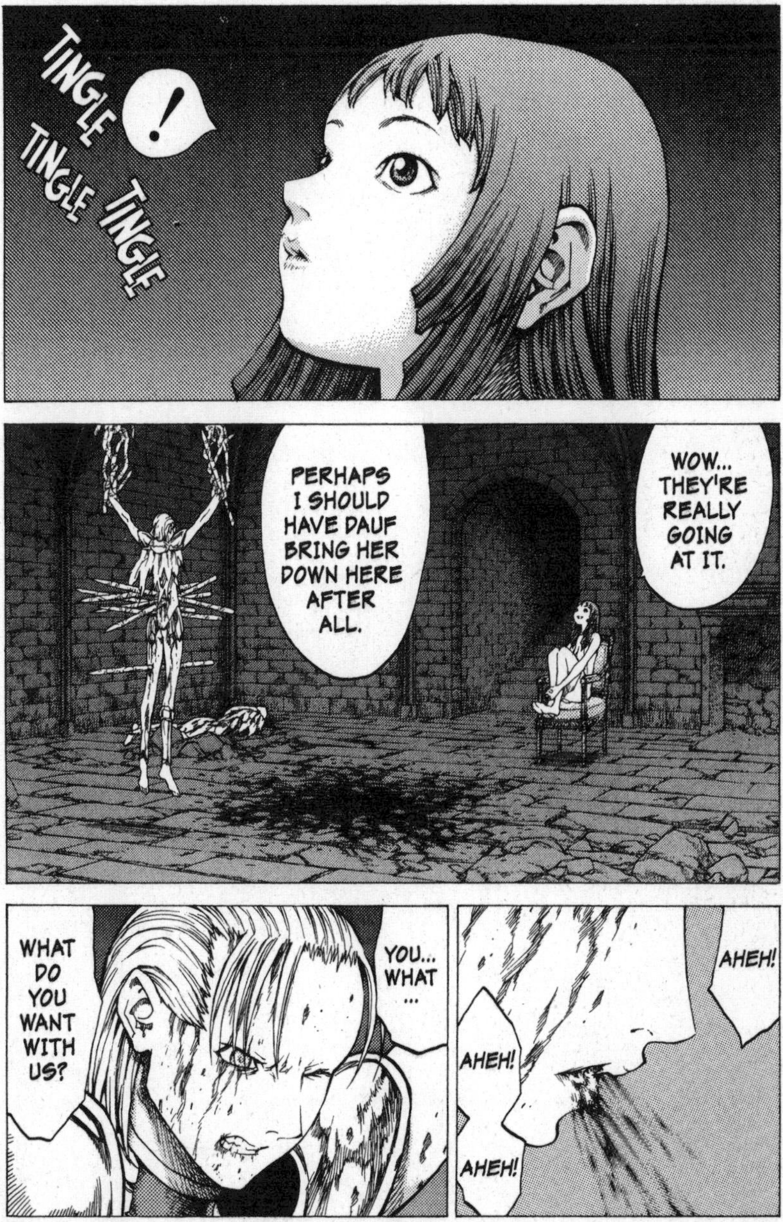
!
TINGLE
TINGLE TINGLE TINGLE
WOW... THEY'RE REALLY GOING AT IT.
PERHAPS I SHOULD HAVE DAUF BRING HER DOWN HERE AFTER ALL.
YOU... WHAT ...
WHAT DO YOU WANT WITH US?
AHEH!
AHEH!
AHEH!

OH, THAT'S SECRET!

BUT I'LL TELL YOU... IF YOU AWAKEN AND JOIN US.

SNICKER

WHO WOULD WANT TO JOIN MONSTERS?

YOU'RE CRAZY!

WHAT'S SO FUNNY?

AWAKENED BEINGS AND HALF YOMA AREN'T REALLY ALL THAT DIFFERENT.

THE ONLY DIFFERENCE IS... WHICH ONE HAS A FREE WILL?

IN THE EYES OF THE COMMON PEOPLE, YOU'RE A MONSTER, AREN'T YOU?

WELL...

ONE THING IS FOR CERTAIN ...

THE FACT THAT BOTH OF THEM ARE NO LONGER HUMAN.

YOU'RE HATED AND REVILED YOUR WHOLE LIFE.

IT SEEMS RATHER STUPID, REALLY.

AND THE HUMANS DON'T EVEN THANK YOU.

YOU'RE CAST OUT BY HUMANS, YOU'RE NO LONGER HUMAN, YET YOU FIGHT FOR HUMANS.

AND WHEN YOUR WORK IS FINISHED, YOU THROW AWAY YOUR OWN LIFE.

DON'T YOU THINK IT'S SILLY?

READ THIS WAY

OF COURSE WE'RE A DIFFER-ENT SPECIES THAN THE HUMANS.
ONCE YOU SEE THAT, EVERYTHING ELSE BECOMES EASY TO ACCEPT.
DO YOU SHED TEARS FOR THE COWS, THE PIGS, THE SHEEP OR THE BIRDS THAT HUMANS FEED ON?
OF COURSE NOT.
AND WHY NOT? BECAUSE THEY'RE A DIFFER-ENT SPECIES.
IT'S JUST NATURE.
IT'S JUST LOGIC.
IT'S JUST PROVIDENCE.
WELL?
AM I WRONG?
THANK YOU FOR SHARING YOUR OPIN-IONS.
IT'S NOT THAT I DON'T UNDER-STAND YOUR ARGU-MENT...
!
YOUR CURRENT THINKING IS WHAT'S UNNATURAL.

THAT MAKES ME WANT TO HAVE YOU JOIN US EVEN MORE.

I LIKE IT WHEN YOU TALK LIKE THAT.

THAT'S THE ONE TRUTH INSIDE ME.

BUT SINCE I WAS BORN A HUMAN, I LIVE FOR HUMANS.

GAAA AAAA

OW...

OW OW OW.

WHA...

GAAAA
THAT LAST ONE HURT.
IT REALLY STUNG.
ALL RIGHT, YOU.
TIME TO PAY THE PIPER.
NO ...
IT CAN'T BE...

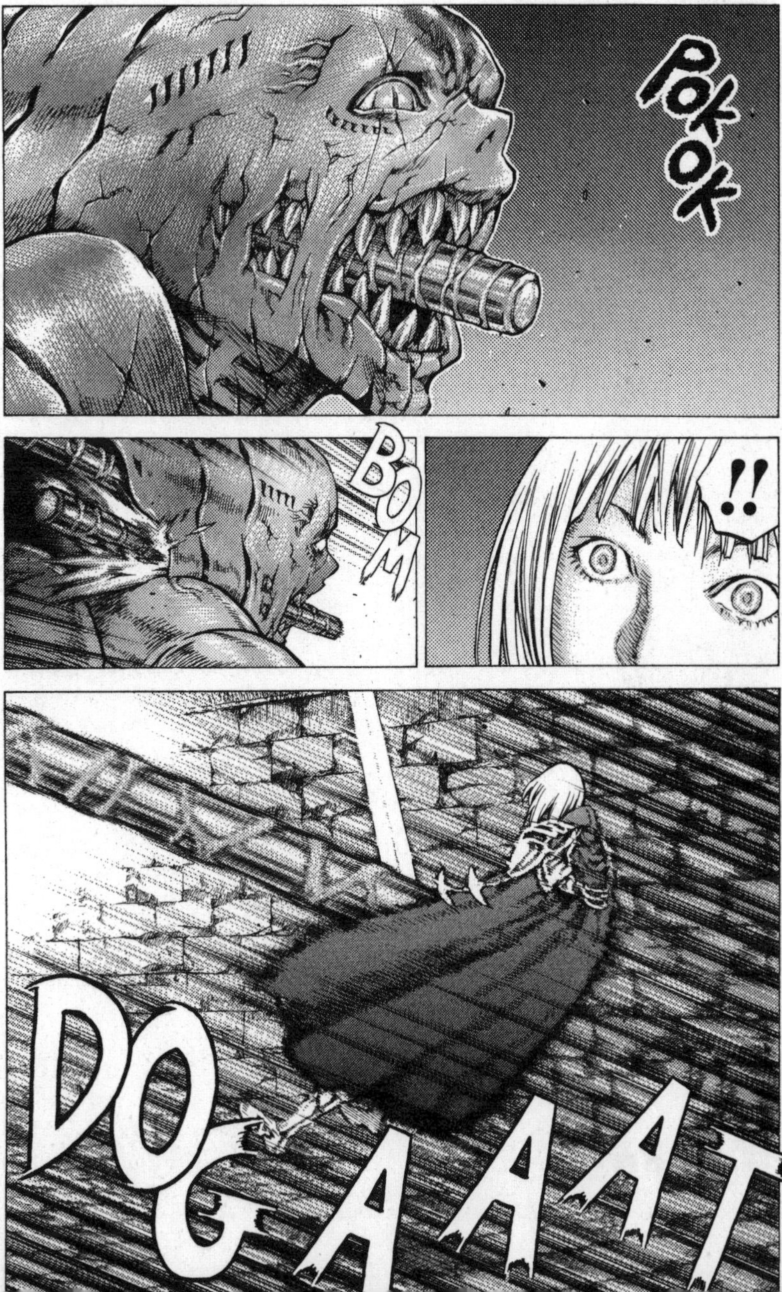
POKOK
BOM
!!
DOGAAAT

READ THIS WAY

DOGAAAT
AGH!
ARGH!
DOGAT
GAN GAN
GAN GAN
UH ...
BIKI
BIKI BIKI BIKI
UH ...
UH ...

READ THIS WAY

!
UH ...
UH ...
SURPRISED?
IT'S HARDER TO FIX CRUSHED BONES THAN IT IS TO REATTACH A SEVERED LIMB.
CLUMP
!
MUUUU
AGH ...
AH ...
NOW, LET'S GET BACK TO PEELIN' YOU...
AND SEEIN' IF YOU'RE MAN OR WOMAN.

WELL, WELL, WELL ...
!
HUH?
AND HERE I WAS SO PLEASED WITH MYSELF ...
...FOR FINDING YOU SO QUICKLY.
GASHAK
GASHAK
GASHAK
!
OH MY!
LOOKS LIKE WE'VE GOT OUR-SELVES A STRONG ONE NOW.

READ THIS WAY

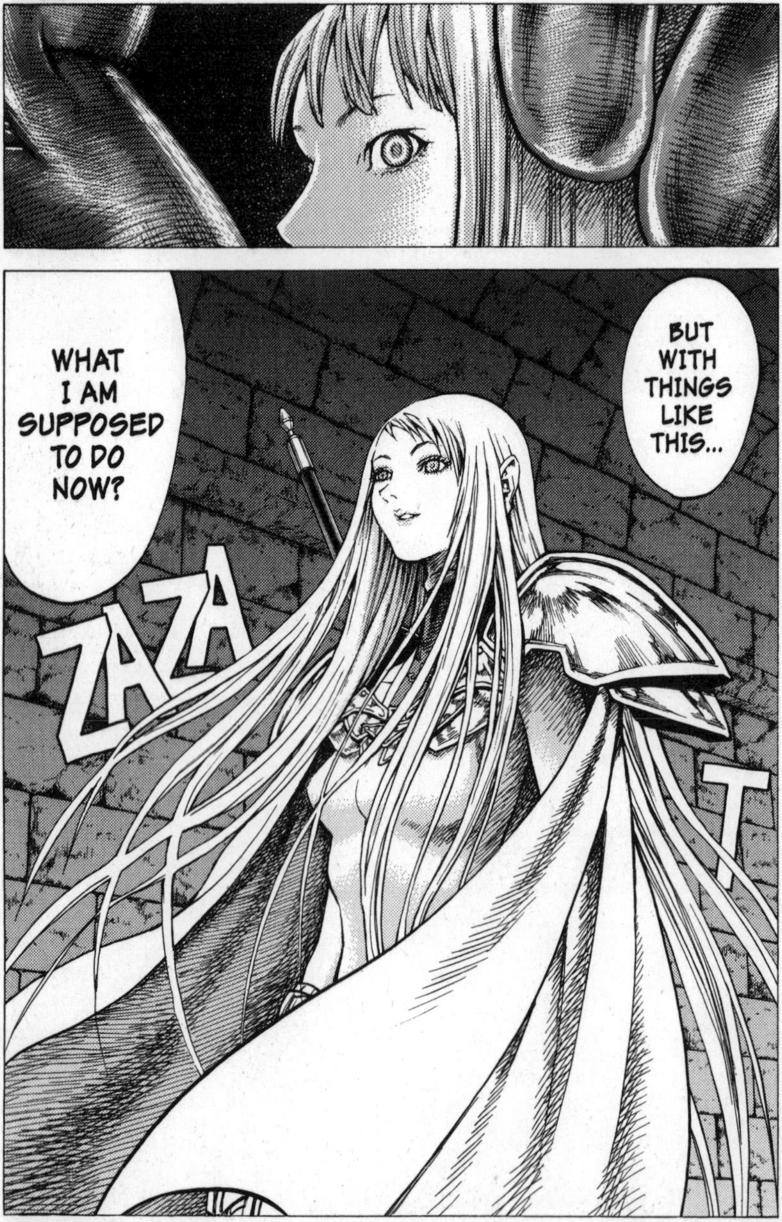

BUT WITH THINGS LIKE THIS...
WHAT I AM SUPPOSED TO DO NOW?
ZAZA
T

クレイモア
Claymore™

Scene 44: The Witch's Maw, Part 4

NOW THAT I'VE COME ALL THIS WAY...
ZAT
...I CAN'T JUST LEAVE EMPTY-HANDED.
KASHAK
KASHAK
KASHAK
!
NOT DRAWING YOUR SWORD...
HOW COME?
KASHAK
KASHAK
THAT MARK...
SHE'S ONE OF THE TOP FIVE.

NUMBER 3 IN THE ORGANIZATION ...
GALATEA!
SCENE 44: THE WITCH'S MAW, PART 4

READ THIS WAY

ZUU
HUH?
DOSAT
!!

READ THIS WAY
!!?
YOU'RE LIGHTER THAN YOU LOOK.
YOU NEED TO EAT MORE.
SHE'S ALL I CAME FOR.
I'LL BE ON MY WAY NOW. GOOD-BYE.
ZAT
EH?
TWITCH
WATCH OUT!
HE'LL ...
FWOM

DO
GAAA
EH?
TMP
TMP
TMP

READ
THIS
WAY

HOLD
ON...
BIKI
BIKI
BIKI
BIKI
WHAT
D'YA
THINK
YOU'RE
DOING?
BIKI

GASHAK

TAKE
THIS!
GRAH!!
FWAAA

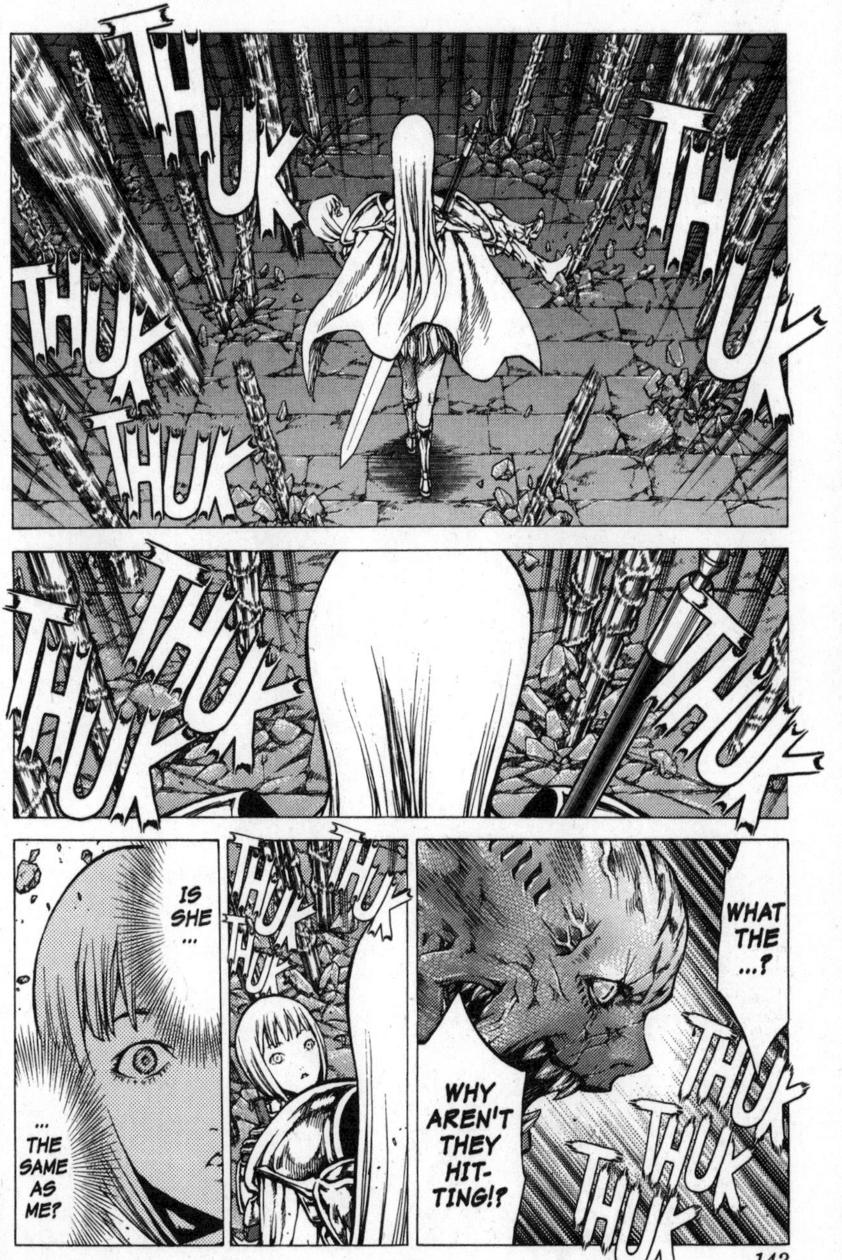

IS SHE
...

...THE SAME AS ME?

WHAT THE ...?

WHY AREN'T THEY HIT-TING!?

READ THIS WAY

NO! IT'S DIFFER-ENT!
SHE'S NOT MOVING HERSELF OUT OF THE WAY AT ALL!
I READ MY OPPO-NENT'S ENERGY AND MOVE BEFORE THE ATTACK.
BUT SHE MAKES THE ATTACK ITSELF DEFLECT!
BUT HOW?
HOW IS THAT POSSI-BLE?
FWOM

DOGAAAA
DOGAGAGA
!
DADADADA
HMM... I UNDER-ESTI-MATED HIM.
PER-HAPS HE'S GOT A BRAIN AFTER ALL.
DADA
GASHAK

READ THIS WAY

YOU AIN'T GOIN' NO-WHERE.
NOBODY MAKES A FOOL OUTTA ME AND GETS AWAY WITH IT.
I'M GONNA KILL YA.
I'M GONNA STRIP YA NAKED, TEAR OFF YOUR HANDS AND FEET, RIP OPEN YOUR BELLY AND SUCK OUT YOUR GUTS.
SHH
YOU SIT HERE AND HEAL YOUR LEGS.
IF YOU CALM DOWN AND RELAX, IT'S NOT THAT HARD.
ZAT
HOW-EVER ...
!
I CAN'T BELIEVE YOU TRIED TO TAKE ON THAT CREATURE.
BE CAREFUL! HE'S GOT A TOUGH HIDE THAT A SWORD CAN'T CUT, AND...
I'M NOT TALK-ING ABOUT THIS ONE.

I MEAN THE OTHER ONE DOWNSTAIRS.

WERE YOU ACTUALLY TRYING TO GET YOURSELF KILLED?

IF YOU CAN ALIGN WAVELENGTHS WITH YOUR OPPONENT'S AURA AT THE CORRECT LOCATION, YOU CAN FIND THEM. YOU'RE A WARRIOR PROFICIENT IN READING YOMA AURAS, AREN'T YOU?

SHE'S DONE A PRETTY GOOD JOB OF HIDING HER AURA, BUT IT'S STILL DETECTABLE.

!!

READ THIS WAY

BUT DON'T WORRY ABOUT THAT FOR NOW.
CONCEN-TRATE ON FIXING YOUR LEGS.
!
DO GAGA GAGA
SINCE MY RODS WON'T HIT YA...
...I'LL JUST HAVE TO SMASH YA!
GO O OO O
DIDN'T YOU SAY YOU WERE GOING TO STRIP ME NAKED, TEAR OFF MY LIMBS, RIP OPEN MY BELLY AND SUCK OUT MY GUTS?
HUH?
WHAT D'YA MEAN?

DO GA AAAT

BWA HA HA HA HA HA HA HA HA HA!

AND SHE THOUGHT SHE COULD TAKE ME!

GALATEA!

READ THIS WAY

FWO M
GAKAAAK
GAKAK
KLAK
KLAK
KLAK
ZA
ZUSHA T

READ THIS WAY

HM?
AH?
I SEE...
A REGU-LAR ATTACK WON'T PIERCE THAT HIDE.
GRAH!
FWOM
SMILE
GURA

DOGAAA
!!?
!
FSSH
GA
SHIN

GAH!
!!
I THOUGHT SO. EVEN A HIDE THIS TOUGH HAS ITS WEAK POINTS.
FSSH
FSSH

SHAK
BA
GAH!
GRAAAH!!
YOU ...
WHOSH
FSSH

READ THIS WAY

GRIP
SUKA
ZA
KO K
WHA...
WHAT...
LOOKS LIKE THE ONE TAKING HANDS AND FEET...
...IS GOING TO BE ME.
ZUBAAT

DOSHAAAK
!!
MY GOD!
SO THIS IS HOW STRONG NUMBER THREE IS.
BUT HOW DOES SHE FIGHT LIKE THAT?
IT'S LIKE SHE CAN MANIPULATE HER OPPONENT AS SHE WILLS.
GAH!
AGH!
AGH ...
AH ...

READ THIS WAY

YOU... CUT ME.
LOOK.
LOOK WHAT YOU DID.
SOB
SOB
STOP YOUR WHIN-ING.
GA SHAK
IT MAKES YOUR FACE EVEN UGLIER.
A FOOL.
!
HE REALLY IS A FOOL.
AND THAT'S WHY...
I DON'T THINK I'LL EVER BE ABLE TO TAKE MUCH PRIDE IN HIM AS MY MAN.

クレイモア
Claymore™

Scene 45: The Witch's Maw, Part 5

HMP...
YOU SHOWED UP SOONER THAN I EXPECTED.
HEY, DAUF.
WHAT ARE YOU DOING? ONLY ONE OPPONENT, AND YOU'VE ALREADY LOST A HAND.
!
BUT... BUT...
MY PUNCHES WEREN'T HITTIN' HER...
SO...
SOB SOB SOB
WHAT ARE YOU SAYING? THERE'S NO WAY YOU COULDN'T HIT HER.
DON'T BE STUPID.
NO... REALLY!
SO I...
SIGH!
ALL RIGHT THEN. I'LL TEACH YOU HOW TO PUNCH SO YOU WON'T MISS HER.
GAH!
SO HIT HER NEXT TIME, OKAY?

USE ALL YOUR STRENGTH.
AND HIT HER WITH ALL YOU'VE GOT.
SCENE 45: THE WITCH'S MAW, PART 5

READ THIS WAY

!
BUT... I JUST TOLD YOU...
THAT'S WHAT I BEEN TRYIN' TO DO.
BUT IT JUST AIN'T WORKIN'.
JUST TRY IT AGAIN, OKAY?
IF YOU MISS THIS TIME, I'M LEAVING YOU.
NO ...
NO ... NOT THAT ...
DAMN ...
DAMN IT.
BIKI
BIKI
BIKI

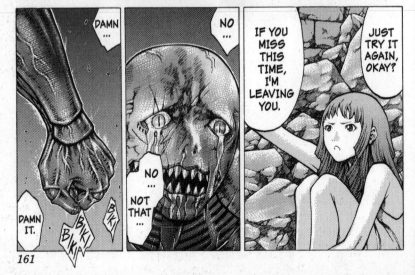

DAMN.
BIKI BIKI
DAMN. DAMN.
BIKI BIKI
!
TINGLE TINGLE
YOU...
BIKI BIKI BIKI
IT'S YOUR FAULT!
TINGLE TINGLE TINGLE
FSH

DOGAAAT
THIS TIME I DIDN'T MISS.
HUH?
!

GAH!
FSSH
TMP
DOGAAT
FSSH
BAKO
GRAAAAH!!
DOGAAT

READ THIS WAY

I JUST MADE DAUF EXERT HIS REAL POWER, THAT'S ALL.

ME? I DIDN'T DO ANY-THING.

YOU ...

WHAT DID YOU DO?

DOING THAT, SHE CAN HARMONIZE WITH HER OPPONENT AND CONTROL THEIR MOTIONS.

YOUR FRIEND'S SPECIALTY IS TO READ THROUGH YOMA AURA AND DISCRIM-INATE DOWN TO THE SMALLEST PART.

SHE CATCHES HER OPPONENT OFF GUARD, AIMS FOR WHERE THEIR AWARENESS IS WEAK, AND PUTTING HER OWN ENERGY IN HARMONY, MOVES THEM JUST A LITTLE BIT.

WELL, I CAN'T GO SO FAR AS TO SAY "CON-TROL."

READ THIS WAY

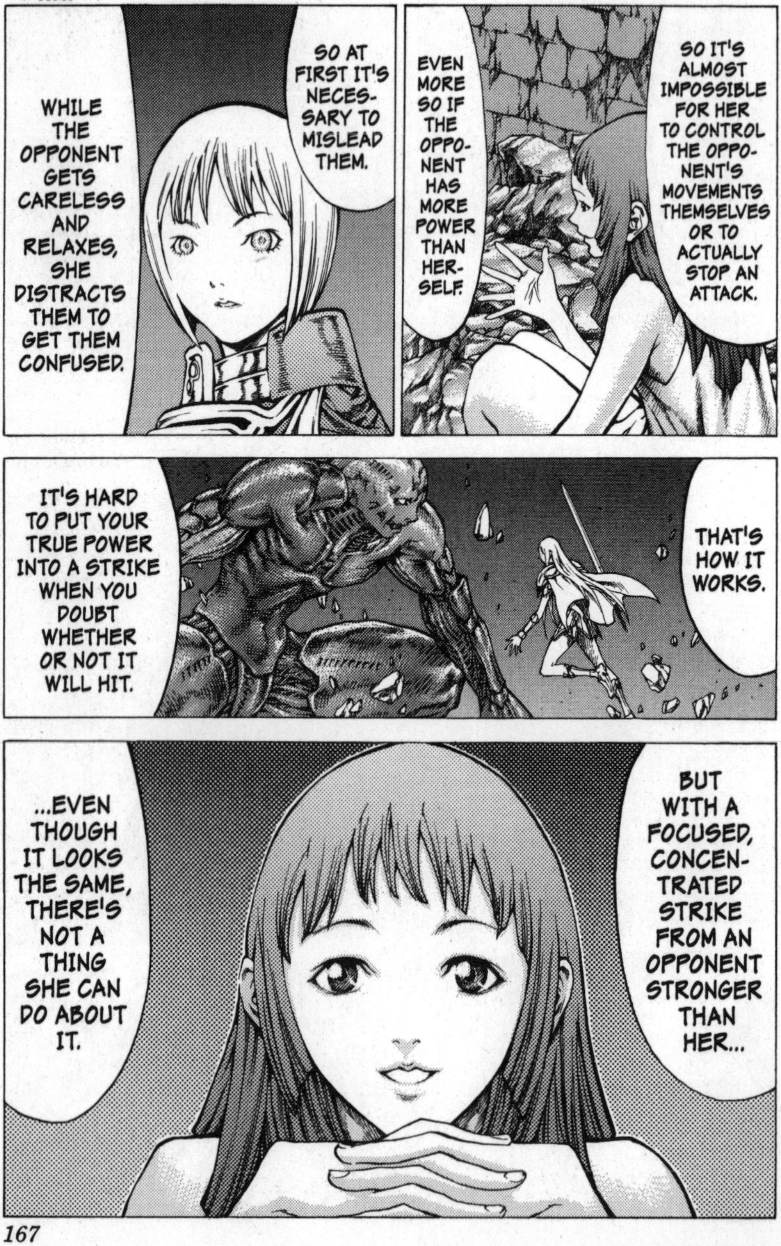

SO IT'S ALMOST IMPOSSIBLE FOR HER TO CONTROL THE OPPONENT'S MOVEMENTS THEMSELVES OR TO ACTUALLY STOP AN ATTACK.
EVEN MORE SO IF THE OPPONENT HAS MORE POWER THAN HERSELF.
SO AT FIRST IT'S NECESSARY TO MISLEAD THEM.
WHILE THE OPPONENT GETS CARELESS AND RELAXES, SHE DISTRACTS THEM TO GET THEM CONFUSED.
THAT'S HOW IT WORKS.
IT'S HARD TO PUT YOUR TRUE POWER INTO A STRIKE WHEN YOU DOUBT WHETHER OR NOT IT WILL HIT.
BUT WITH A FOCUSED, CONCENTRATED STRIKE FROM AN OPPONENT STRONGER THAN HER...
...EVEN THOUGH IT LOOKS THE SAME, THERE'S NOT A THING SHE CAN DO ABOUT IT.

GA CHANG
DO OM
DOBA
FSSH

DOGAGAGA
OW.
OW.
OW.
!!?
BAKO
ARG!
FWNSH
DOGAGA
!!
SHHP
GRR...

DOSHAA
GALATEA!!
GAH!
OW OW ...
GASHAN
YOU'RE GONNA PAY FOR THIS.
!!
GET OUT OF THERE!
AH ...
SHHP

DOGAAAA
AAGH!
GYEH.
GOT 'ER!
WHERE SHOULD I HIT HER NEXT?
DA... DAMN.
THE ONLY THING I CAN DO IS HIT HIM IN THE JAW...
IT'S OVER, ISN'T IT?

DO
OM
!
WELL, WHAT'S THIS?
IT'S GOOD THAT YOU RELEASED ENOUGH POWER TO HEAL YOUR LEGS...
BUT NOW YOU'VE CROSSED YOUR LIMITS.
BIKI
BIKI
BIKI

DO
BAAA
NEXT ...
GAA
DO
I'LL CRUSH HER HEAD!
UGH ...
DOGAAAA

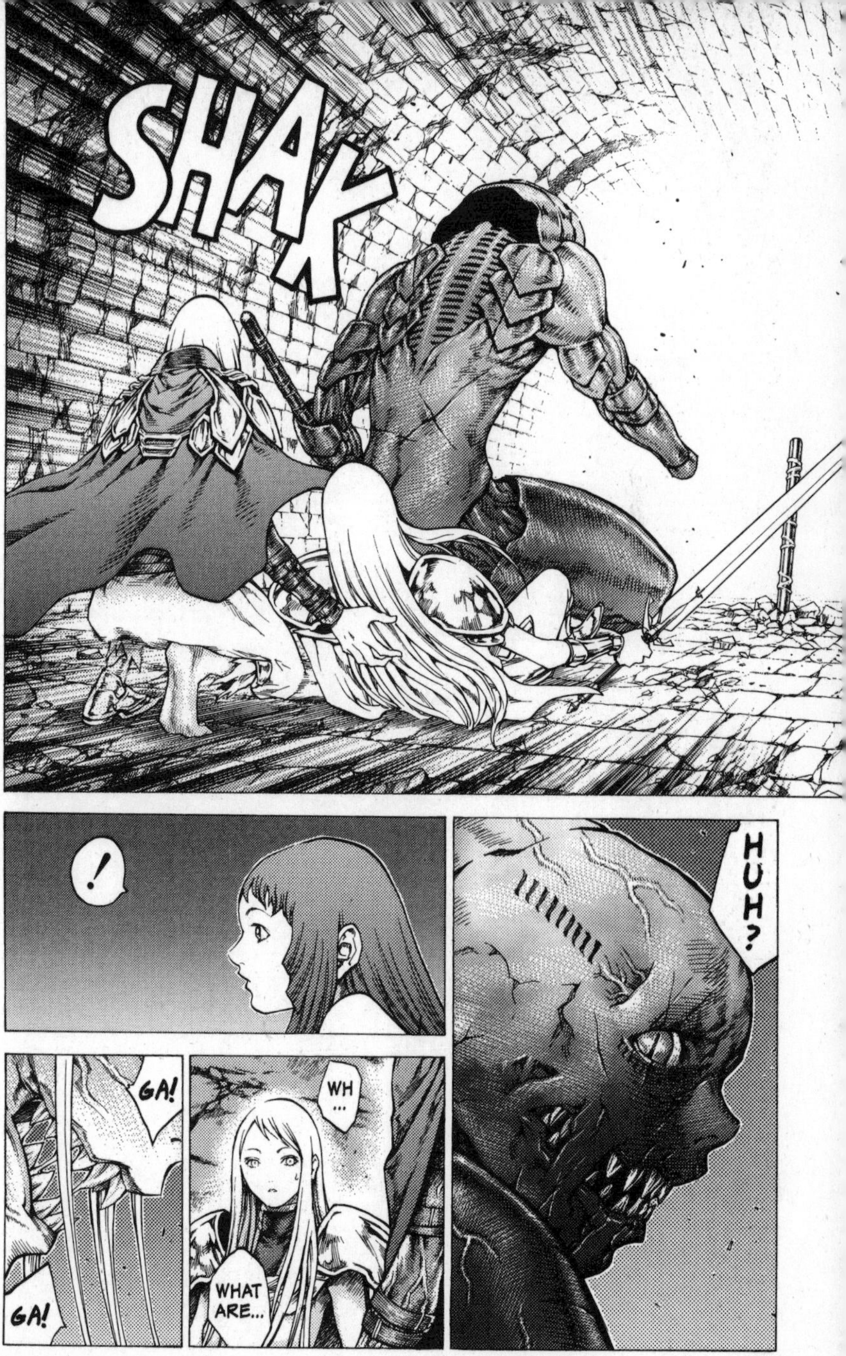
SHAK
HUH?
!
WH...
WHAT ARE...
GA!
GA!

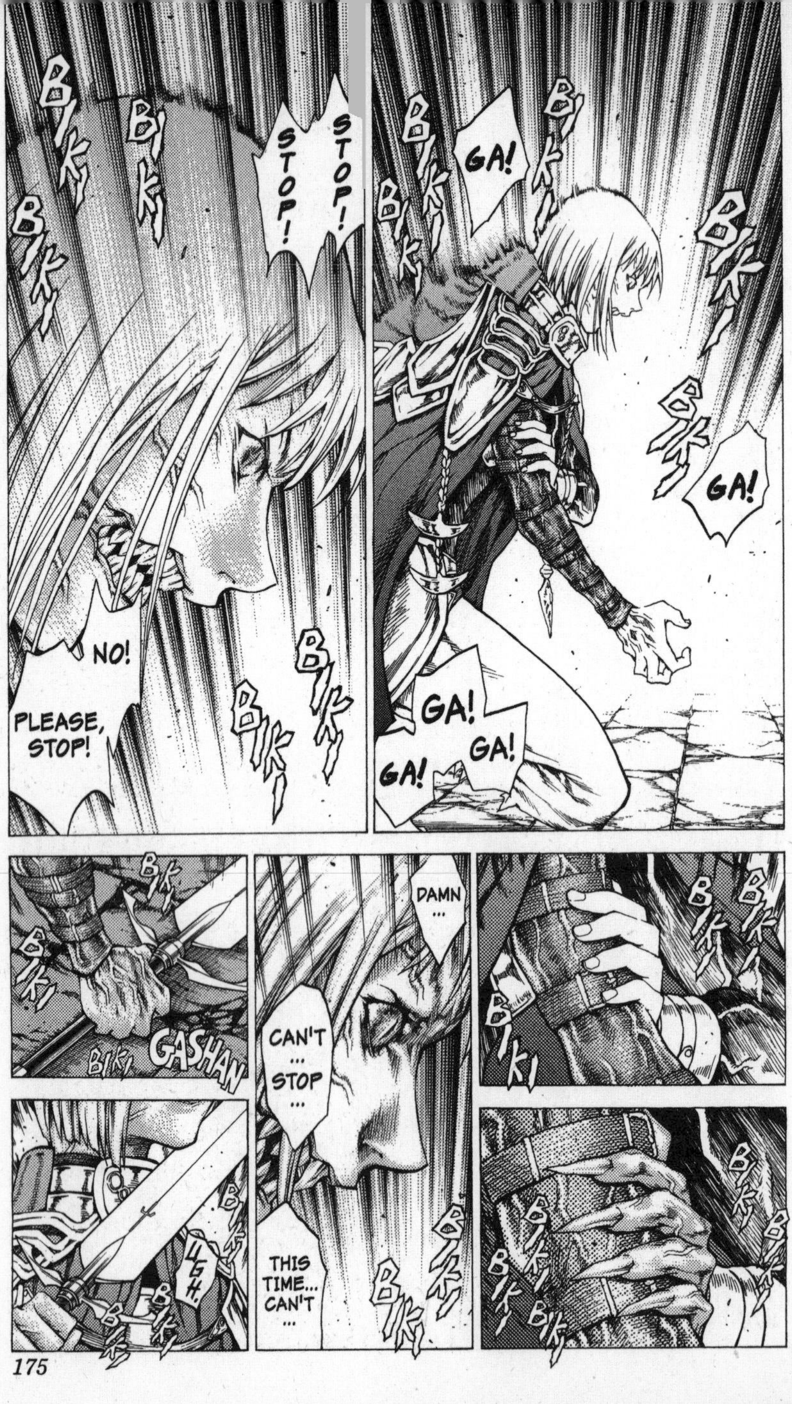

175

HUH !?

F
W
U
U

BUT THAT IT COULD ACTUALLY BE DONE...

I THOUGHT IT WAS JUST MY IMAGINATION WHEN I FELT IT BACK IN THE MOUNTAINS.

!

I THOUGHT YOU MIGHT BE TRYING TO BRING YOURSELF BACK AFTER CROSSING YOUR LIMITS...

MY GOD...

READ THIS WAY

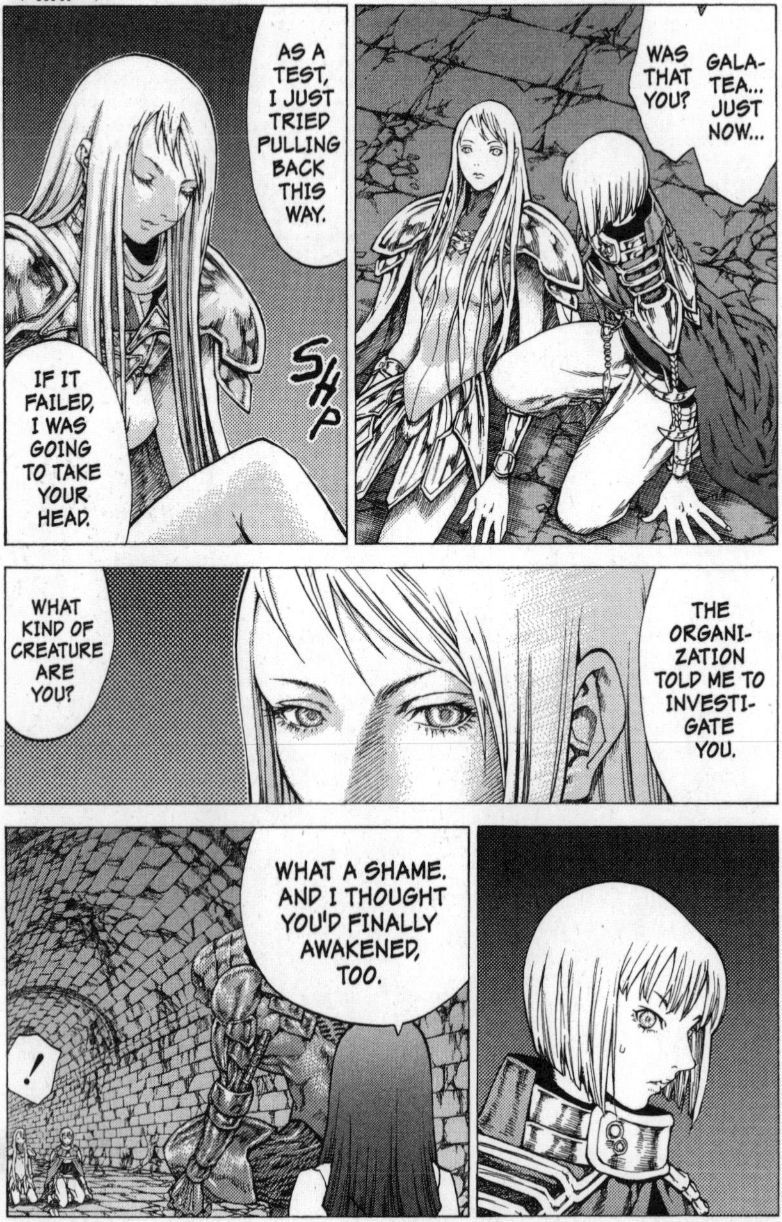

GALA-TEA... JUST NOW...
WAS THAT YOU?
SHP
AS A TEST, I JUST TRIED PULLING BACK THIS WAY.
IF IT FAILED, I WAS GOING TO TAKE YOUR HEAD.
THE ORGANI-ZATION TOLD ME TO INVESTI-GATE YOU.
WHAT KIND OF CREATURE ARE YOU?
WHAT A SHAME. AND I THOUGHT YOU'D FINALLY AWAKENED, TOO.
!

I'VE DEVELOPED A LIKING FOR BOTH OF YOU.

A MYSTERIOUS WARRIOR PULLED BACK FROM AWAKENING BY A HIGH-RANKING NUMBER...

...JOIN MY GROUP.

I'LL LET YOU TWO...

DON'T WORRY ABOUT IT.

HOW IS YOUR WOUND?

AS A DEFENSIVE STYLE WARRIOR, I HEAL FAST.

HUFF

HUFF

HUFF

READ THIS WAY

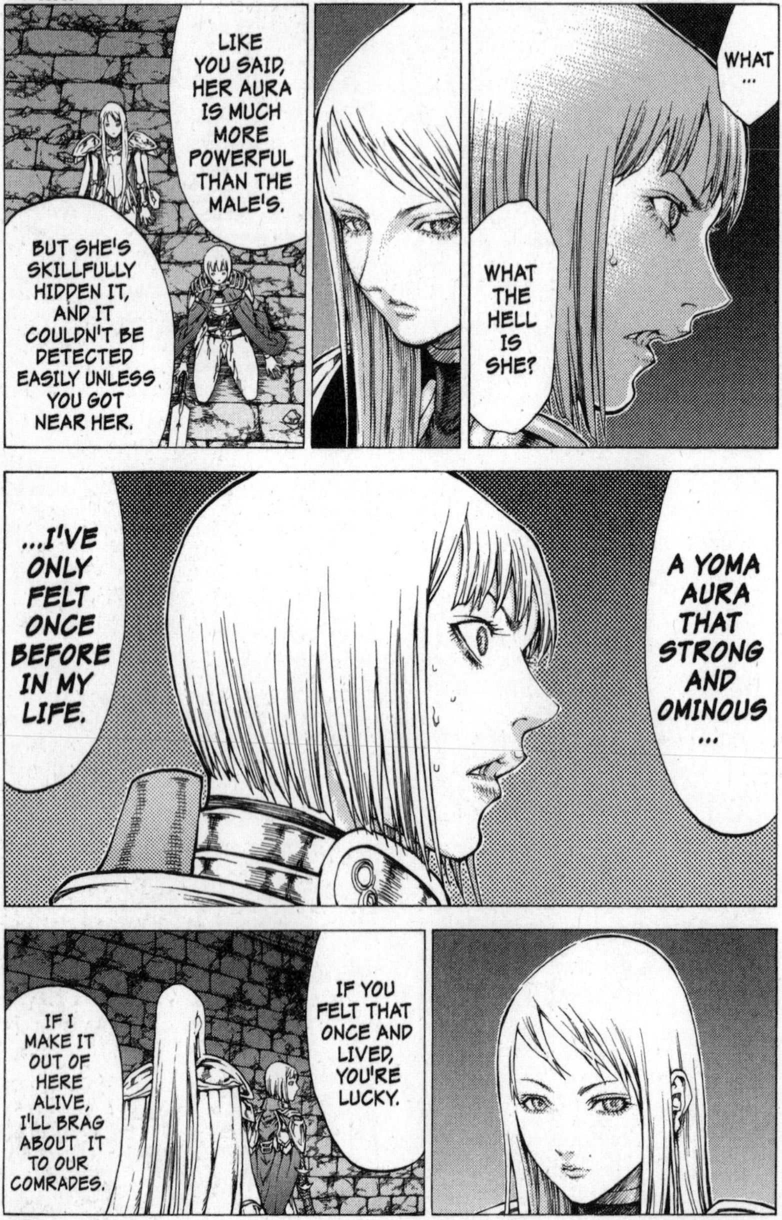
WHAT ...
WHAT THE HELL IS SHE?
LIKE YOU SAID, HER AURA IS MUCH MORE POWERFUL THAN THE MALE'S.
BUT SHE'S SKILLFULLY HIDDEN IT, AND IT COULDN'T BE DETECTED EASILY UNLESS YOU GOT NEAR HER.
A YOMA AURA THAT STRONG AND OMINOUS ...
...I'VE ONLY FELT ONCE BEFORE IN MY LIFE.
IF YOU FELT THAT ONCE AND LIVED, YOU'RE LUCKY.
IF I MAKE IT OUT OF HERE ALIVE, I'LL BRAG ABOUT IT TO OUR COMRADES.

READ THIS WAY

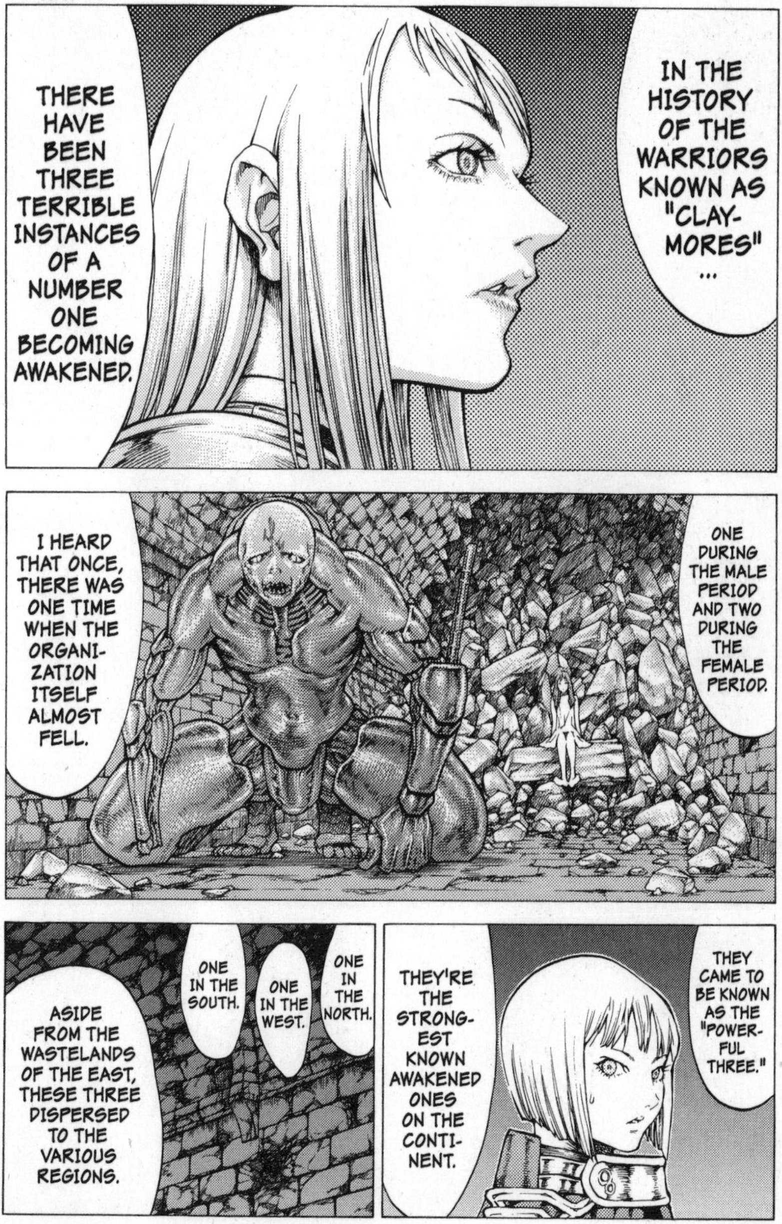

IN THE HISTORY OF THE WARRIORS KNOWN AS "CLAYMORES"...
THERE HAVE BEEN THREE TERRIBLE INSTANCES OF A NUMBER ONE BECOMING AWAKENED.
ONE DURING THE MALE PERIOD AND TWO DURING THE FEMALE PERIOD.
I HEARD THAT ONCE, THERE WAS ONE TIME WHEN THE ORGANIZATION ITSELF ALMOST FELL.
THEY CAME TO BE KNOWN AS THE "POWERFUL THREE."
THEY'RE THE STRONGEST KNOWN AWAKENED ONES ON THE CONTINENT.
ONE IN THE NORTH.
ONE IN THE WEST.
ONE IN THE SOUTH.
ASIDE FROM THE WASTELANDS OF THE EAST, THESE THREE DISPERSED TO THE VARIOUS REGIONS.

READ THIS WAY

KNOWING OF EACH OTHERS' POWER, THEY TRY TO AVOID UNNECES-SARY CONTACT.
EVER SINCE, THE THREE HAVE NOT APPEARED OPENLY, AND HAVE COME TO BE CALLED THE CREATURES OF THE ABYSS.
IF THEY HAD STAYED SLUMBERING QUIETLY IN THE DEPTHS, IT WOULD HAVE BEEN GOOD.
BUT RECENTLY, WE'VE HEARD THAT ALL THREE OF THEM HAVE BEGUN UNUSUAL ACTIVI-TIES.
EACH ONE HAS STARTED GATHERING AWAKENED ONES TOGETHER.
IT'S AS THOUGH THEY ARE EACH BUILDING ARMIES FOR WAR.
SMIRK
AND NOW I SHOULD LIKE YOUR AN-SWER.
WHAT ON EARTH ARE YOU TRYING TO DO?

THE FIRST NUMBER ONE FEMALE WARRIOR IN THE HISTORY OF THE ORGANI-ZATION.
THE YOUNGEST WARRIOR IN HISTORY TO EVER REACH THAT PEAK, AND THE YOUNGEST WARRIOR TO EVER RELEASE SUCH POWER.

READ THIS WAY

CREATURE OF THE ABYSS ...
RIFUL OF THE WEST.

CREATURE OF THE ABYSS?
RIFUL OF THE WEST?
YOU'RE WELL INFORMED.
QUITE A THING, FOR SOMEONE SO YOUNG.
IT'S NOT THAT WE'VE BEEN AVOIDING CONTACT WITH EACH OTHER.
IT'S JUST THAT WE DIDN'T END UP IN THE SAME PLACE.
TO BE HONEST, IT WAS RATHER BORING.
EAT AND SLEEP, EAT AND SLEEP, DAY AFTER DAY.

READ THIS WAY

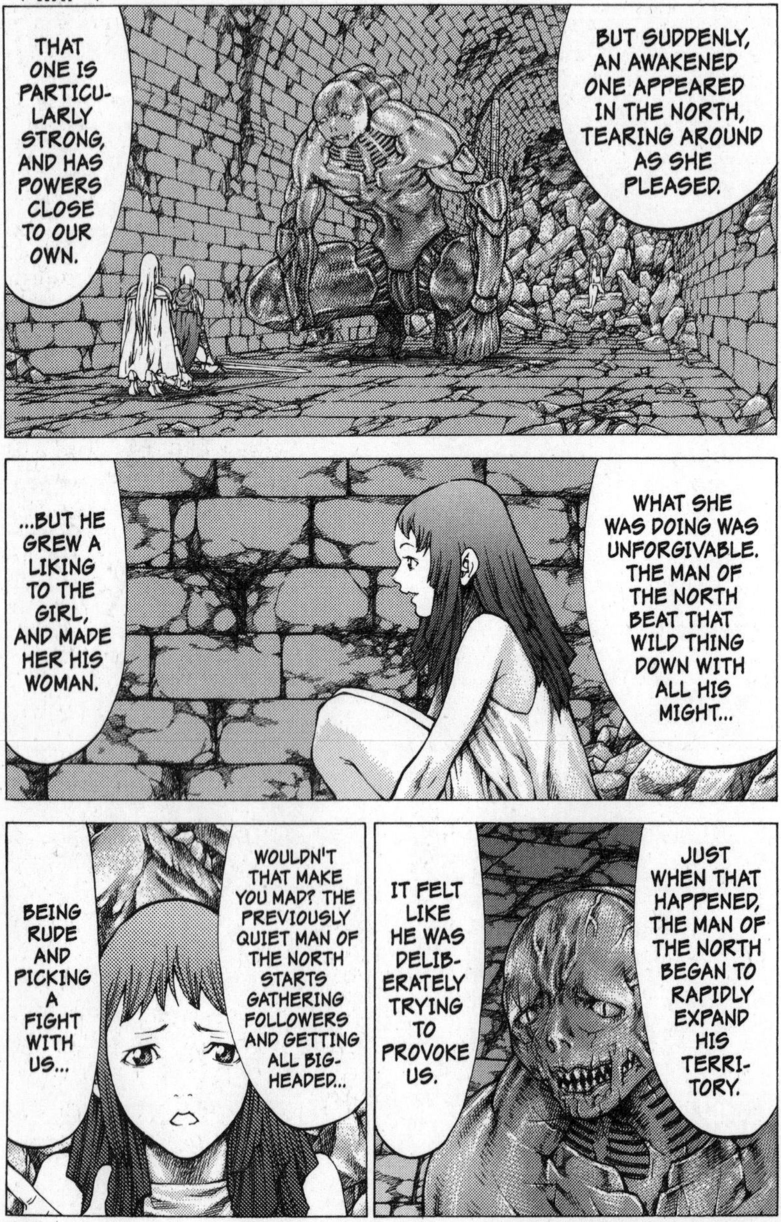
BUT SUDDENLY, AN AWAKENED ONE APPEARED IN THE NORTH, TEARING AROUND AS SHE PLEASED.
THAT ONE IS PARTICU-LARLY STRONG, AND HAS POWERS CLOSE TO OUR OWN.
WHAT SHE WAS DOING WAS UNFORGIVABLE. THE MAN OF THE NORTH BEAT THAT WILD THING DOWN WITH ALL HIS MIGHT...
...BUT HE GREW A LIKING TO THE GIRL, AND MADE HER HIS WOMAN.
JUST WHEN THAT HAPPENED, THE MAN OF THE NORTH BEGAN TO RAPIDLY EXPAND HIS TERRI-TORY.
IT FELT LIKE HE WAS DELIB-ERATELY TRYING TO PROVOKE US.
WOULDN'T THAT MAKE YOU MAD? THE PREVIOUSLY QUIET MAN OF THE NORTH STARTS GATHERING FOLLOWERS AND GETTING ALL BIG-HEADED...
BEING RUDE AND PICKING A FIGHT WITH US...

I WAS GETTING BORED, AND IT MIGHT BE FUN.

WELL, ANYWAY, IF IT'S A FIGHT HE WANTS, WE'LL GIVE HIM ONE.

RIGHT NOW, WE DON'T HAVE NEARLY ENOUGH FOR BATTLE STRENGTH.

SO THAT'S WHY I'M GATHERING FOLLOWERS, TOO.

RIGHT NOW IT APPEARS THAT SHE'S FORGOTTEN THE DAMAGE THE MAN OF THE NORTH DID TO HER WHEN THEY FOUGHT, BUT...

STILL, THE THING THAT MAKES ME THE MOST ANGRY IS THAT GIRL WHO WAS RUNNING AMOK.

...

READ THIS WAY

THEY SAY THAT IN THE TOWNS SHE ATTACKED, SHE COMPLETELY DESTROYED EVERY-THING.
YET SHE NEVER LAID A HAND ON THE YOUNG GIRLS.
!
WH...
WHAT?
SHE'S A STRANGE ONE. EVEN THOUGH SHE TEARS OUT THE GUTS OF EVERY-ONE ELSE IN THE VILLAGE...
SHE DOESN'T MAKE A SINGLE WOUND ON THE YOUNG GIRLS.
IT'S ALMOST LIKE...
SHE DOESN'T EVEN NOTICE THE YOUNG GIRLS AT ALL.

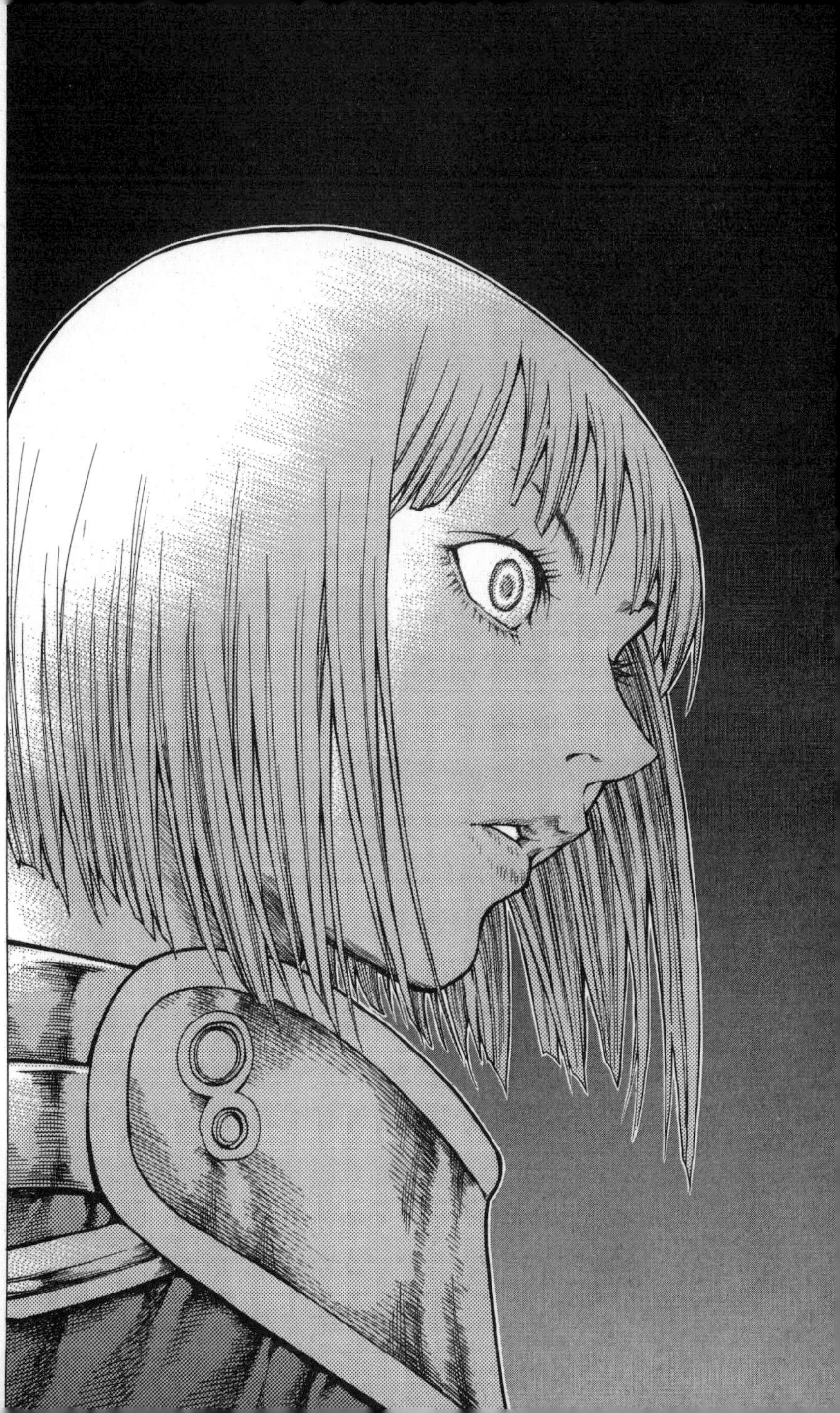

READ THIS WAY

WHERE...
!
...IS SHE ...
WHERE IS...
...THAT BEAST?
BIKI
WHAT DID YOU SAY?
YOUR VOICE IS SO SMALL, I CAN'T HEAR YOU.
WHAM
WHAT IS THE NAME OF THE MAN OF THE NORTH?
I'M GOING TO KILL HIS WOMAN!
FWSSH
END OF VOL. 8: THE WITCH'S MAW

IN THE NEXT VOLUME

A larger plot is revealed when it's discovered that a powerful Awakened male warrior is building an army of Awakened Ones and Yoma in the northern lands. Clare, under threat of death for having escaped the Organization, is told that she'll be forgiven if she joins a group of warriors headed north. But is this a chance at redemption, or a suicide mission?

Available Now

HOSHIN ENGI

$7.99

MANGA
ON SALE NOW!

WHO IS BEHIND THE
MYSTERIOUS HOSHIN
PROJECT?

On sale at:
www.shonenjump.com
Also available at your local
bookstore and comic store.

HOSHIN ENGI © 1996 by Ryu Fujisaki/SHUEISHA Inc.

BLACK CAT
BLACK CAT
BLACK CAT 1 Kentaro Yabuki
SHONEN JUMP MANGA
Story & Art by
Kentaro Yabuki
volume 1
$7.99
Manga on sale now!
Crossing paths with bounty hunter Train, also known as "BLACK CAT," is seriously bad luck for criminals!
SHONEN JUMP
BLACK CAT © 2000 by Kentaro Yabuki/SHUEISHA Inc.
On sale at:
www.shonenjump.com
Also available at your local bookstore and comic store.
RATED T+ FOR OLDER TEEN
viz media

SJ ADVANCED
EYESHIELD 21
Gear up for the best bone-crushing slapstick football manga ever!
Manga on sale now!
$7.99
EYESHIELD 21
SHONEN JUMP ADVANCED
1
SHONEN JUMP
ADVANCED
EYESHIELD 21 © 2002 by Riichiro Inagaki, Yusuke Murata/SHUEISHA In
On sale at:
www.shonenjump.com
Also available at your local
RATED T+ FOR OLDER TEEN
viz media

12 rings to raise the dead...
one man to find them
...HAPPY?
ONLY $7.99
ZOMBIEPOWDER.
SHONEN JUMP MANGA
Tite Kubo
volume 1
Manga series on sale now!
ZOMBIEPOWDER.™
viz media
ww.viz.com
MBIEPOWDER. © 1999 by Tite Kubo/SHUEISHA Inc.
RATED T+ FOR OLDER TEEN
SJ
On sale at:
www.shonenjump.com
Also available at your local bookstore and comic store.
SHONEN JUMP MANGA

CAN LIGHT LEAD THE WORLD OUT OF DARKNESS?
Manga on sale now!
SHONEN JUMP ADVANCED
TSUGUMI OHBA
TAKESHI OBATA
$7.99
SHONEN JUMP ADVANCED
DEATH NOTE © 2003 by Tsugumi Ohba, Takeshi Obata/SHUEISH
On sale at:
www.shonenjump.com
Also available at your local
RATED T+ FOR OLDER TEEN

Taking on the afterlife
one soul at a time...

ONLY
$7.95

Manga series on sale now!

BLEACH © 2001 by Tite Kubo/SHUEISHA Inc.

NARUTO™
Manga on sale now!
$7.95
NARUTO 1
SHONEN JUMP GRAPHIC NOVEL
Story & Art by Masashi Kishimoto volume 1
Naruto is determined to become the greatest ninja ever!
SHONEN JUMP MANGA
NARUTO © 1999 by Masashi Kishimoto/SHUEISHA Inc.
On sale at:
www.shonenjump.com
Also available at your local bookstore and comic store.
RATED T FOR TEEN
viz media
www.viz.com

Tell us what you think about SHONEN JUMP manga!

Our survey is now available online.
Go to: ***www.SHONENJUMP.com/mangasurvey***

Help us make our product offering better!

THE REAL ACTION STARTS IN...

SHONEN JUMP
THE WORLD'S MOST POPULAR MANGA
www.shonenjump.com

SJ ADVANCED

SJ

VIZ media

BLEACH © 2001 by Tite Kubo/SHUEISHA Inc. NARUTO © 1999 by Masashi Kishimoto/SHUEISHA Inc.
DEATH NOTE © 2003 by Tsugumi Ohba, Takeshi Obata/SHUEISHA Inc. ONE PIECE © 1997 by Eiichiro Oda/SHUEISHA Inc.

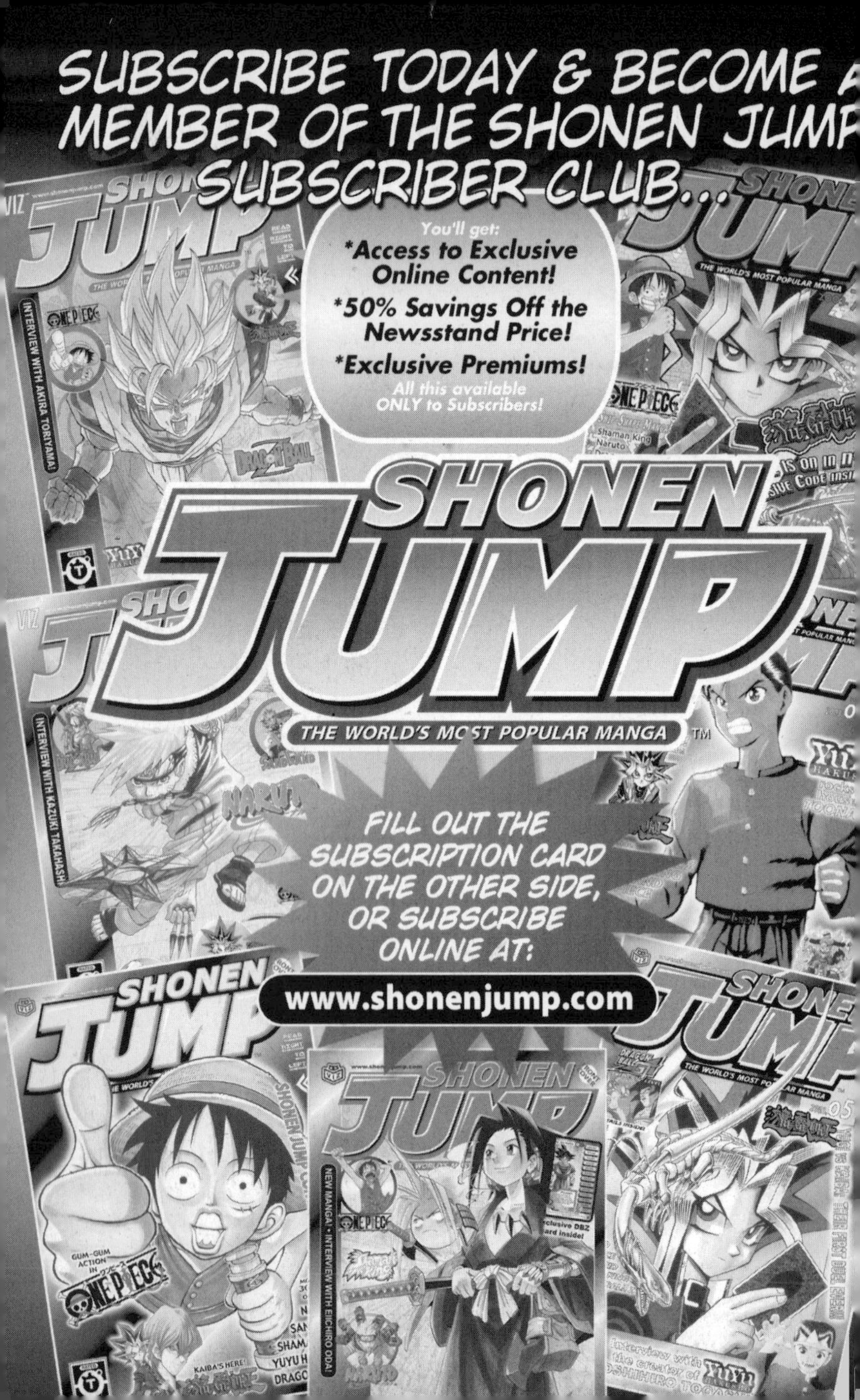
SUBSCRIBE TODAY & BECOME A MEMBER OF THE SHONEN JUMP SUBSCRIBER CLUB...
You'll get:
*Access to Exclusive Online Content!
*50% Savings Off the Newsstand Price!
*Exclusive Premiums!
All this available ONLY to Subscribers!
SHONEN JUMP
THE WORLD'S MOST POPULAR MANGA
FILL OUT THE SUBSCRIPTION CARD ON THE OTHER SIDE, OR SUBSCRIBE ONLINE AT:
www.shonenjump.com

D0985502

Save 50% off the new

SHONEN JUMP™

THE WORLD'S MOST POPULAR MANGA

SUBSCRIBE TODAY and SAVE 50% OFF the cover price PLUS enjoy all the benefits of the SHONEN JUMP SUBSCRIBER CLUB, exclusive online content & special gifts ONLY AVAILABLE to SUBSCRIBERS!

☑ **YES!** Please enter my 1 year subscription (12 issues) to *SHONEN JUMP* at the INCREDIBLY LOW SUBSCRIPTION RATE of $29.95 and sign me up for the SHONEN JUMP Subscriber Club!

Only $29.95!

NAME

ADDRESS

CITY STATE ZIP

E-MAIL ADDRESS

☐ MY CHECK IS ENCLOSED ☐ BILL ME LATER

CREDIT CARD: ☐ VISA ☐ MASTERCARD

ACCOUNT # EXP. DATE

SIGNATURE

CLIP AND MAIL TO

SHONEN JUMP
Subscriptions Service Dept.
P.O. Box 515
Mount Morris, IL 61054-0515

Make checks payable to: **SHONEN JUMP.**
Canada add US $12. No foreign orders. Allow 6-8 weeks for delivery.

P6SJGN YU-GI-OH! © 1996 by Kazuki Takahashi / SHUEISHA Inc.